SPRINGBOARD FOR FAITH

Springboard for Faith

Alister McGrath
and
Michael Green

Hodder & Stoughton
LONDON SYDNEY AUCKLAND

British Library Cataloguing in Publication Data.

A catalogue record for this book is available from the British Library

ISBN 0–340–60130–2

Published by Hodder and Stoughton, a division of Hodder and Stoughton Ltd, Mill Road, Dunton Green, Sevenoaks, Kent TN13 2YA
Editorial Office: 47 Bedford Square, London WC1B 3DP

Photoset by Hewer Text Composition Services, Edinburgh
Printed in Great Britain by Cox & Wyman Ltd, Reading

Contents

Foreword

Alister McGrath and Michael Green are among the foremost Christian thinkers in Britain today. Their skills and abilities in theology, teaching and evangelism are well known. In this book they set out to examine why many people are not Christians nowadays – and to show how they can change. To some degree, we Christians are at fault. Our worship may put off people who feel a wistfulness to find God. But we ourselves may feel unready to share Christianity with others, because we are conscious that we do not know our faith well enough. If that is the reason, take heart! This book is for you. It is written for the ordinary church member, and its approach is thoughtful and readable. I am so glad to be able to commend this book, because this Decade of Evangelism will mean very little, if we are not all sharing our faith in ways that our world can understand.

George Carey
Archbishop of Canterbury

Introduction

Almost all books emerge from a stimulus and an occasion. This one certainly does! The stimulus has been a personal friendship between the authors, and a profound conviction that the Christian account of the world is not merely relevant, but *true*. Indeed, we are persuaded that it is only relevant because it is true. The occasion was the first Springboard conference in December 1992, which we led jointly. Dr McGrath had recently published his outstanding book on apologetics, *Bridge-Building* (IVP). An important conference on the same subject had been hosted a little earlier by Bishops Lesslie Newbigin and Hugh Montefiore, entitled *The Gospel and Our Culture*, which sought to regain the academic high ground at a period of massive cultural shift and change in our understanding of the nature of human knowledge. It has subsequently led to the production of the video *It's No Good Shouting!* and the book *The Gospel and Contemporary Culture*. Clearly a new day is dawning, a day of renewed confidence in the truth of the Christian story.

It is, in fact, a fascinating time to be alive. The dogmas of the Enlightenment, which have dominated Western thought for two centuries, are in full retreat. The barrenness of materialism is evident. The hunger for spirituality is very clear. Even if people have yet to discover fully the spirituality of historic Christianity, they are aware that there is a spiritual dimension to life which is not being satisfied. We are standing at one of the turning points of human thought.

At such a time as this, it is vitally important to understand why so many people in the West are not Christians, and how thoughtful, believing Christians can reach out to them in a way that is loving, attractive and reasonable. This is what we have tried to do in this book. It is directed to the ordinary Christian in the pew, in the first instance, although it is our hope that clergy and theological students will find its ideas and methods helpful.

We are well aware that we have skated over a number of important issues in the interest of clarity and simplicity. We propose to remedy this in due course, by developing this book in depth and length to yield a substantial work on its themes. This will take time. Yet this smaller book is needed *now*. It seemed to us to be important at this critical juncture to put this basic tool into the hands of Christians who want to share their faith with others, but are puzzled about how to go about it. In this Decade of Evangelism there are thousands of Christians like this, and we long to offer them a tool which they can use. It is our prayer that this will prove a help to many.

We trust that it will not only strengthen confidence in the truth of the gospel, but give some helpful suggestions as to how we may commend it to others in terms which make sense to them. And we are very grateful to Carolyn Armitage of Hodder & Stoughton for the alacrity with which she has taken up our suggestions, and made them into a book which is widely available at a price that most people can afford.

May God make us all more confident, humble, and enthusiastic sharers of the Easter faith. Jesus lives – Alleluia!

Michael Green
Easter, 1993

1

Starting Where People Are

One of the greatest changes in the history of the Western Church has taken place in the last generation. It was not all that long ago that the churches saw themselves as having chiefly pastoral and prophetic roles. They were concerned with caring for the wellbeing of their congregations and communities, and standing up for justice and integrity when these were seen to be threatened. Yet now things are changing – fast. Something new has been added to these concerns. Rather than displace them, it is coming to be seen as vital to the effective continuation of these roles in the future. The new concern is now being seen as essential, if the Christian churches are to play a major role in Western society in the third millennium. The name of this concern? *Evangelism.*

Rediscovering Evangelism

Evangelism. How much the associations of that word have changed! It was not all that long ago that it was associated just with lonely individuals such as the incomparable Billy Graham, with his vast crusades. It was seen as the particular concern – indeed, you could say obsession – of evangelical groups within Christianity. It was something that the mainstream churches need not worry about. The future seemed secure, without this emphasis upon 'witnessing' to people, or 'proclaiming the gospel'. The immediate post-war boom in church attendance and Christian commitment was seen as representing a permanent state of affairs. Many senior church figures denounced evangelism as 'Christian imperialism', seeing it as a hangover from the days of colonialism and empire building. It was a quaint and old-fashioned idea, which would never catch on.

That was yesterday. Today, we have seen a dramatic change of mood. The need for evangelism has been conceded all round – as a matter of urgency. The church establishments have realised that the post-war belief boom was a temporary trend which disguised a growing alienation from Christianity. The situation was not addressed with the seriousness it deserved, and the price of that neglect has been depressingly high. In England, the national Church busied itself with navel gazing, undertaking a major and lengthy reform of canon law. And while it fiddled, tinkering with its internal regulations, a nation lost its faith. The crises of the 1960s arrived. *Time* magazine headlined 'the death of God'. Secularisation hit Western society. Church membership began to decline. In 1952, 2% of the American population claimed no religious affiliation. Ten years later, that figure was virtually unaltered. Today, it stands at 12%, and shows every sign of continuing unchecked. In the 1970s, the mainstream churches began to lose members on a long-term basis. By the late 1980s, the pattern was clear. Those churches committed to evangelism were growing; those which scorned it were declining.

Many were reminded of Hans Christian Andersen's story of the emperor's new clothes, where an illusion is shattered by the insistent questioning of a young boy. The churches' illusion of a safe and assured future was shown up by the litany of decline emerging from recent church attendance statistics. 'If some of my own clergy who go around to their endless committees and yak

and yak away would only get on with the job of trying to convert their own parishioners, I think that we should not be in quite the state of decline that we are.' This remark of Mervyn Stockwood, one of the Anglican Church's most creative, radical bishops of the 1960s, bears witness to the new realism that has settled over Anglicanism.

It comes as no surprise to discover that, in the 1990s, evangelism has gone mainstream. It is no longer the prerogative of any religious party or denomination. Some still refuse to face up to the grim realities, hoping for a turn-around in their fortunes without any effort on their part. But for the most part, a new realism has dawned within the churches. They have realised that they can only maintain an effective pastoral and prophetic role in pluralist Western society on the basis of merited influence – from a position justified on the basis of present numerical strength, rather than increasingly vague past glories. Nostalgia may be a nice experience – but it does nothing to ensure the presence of an effective, caring Christian voice in an increasingly confused and dislocated society. A colleague asked me recently if I believed in evangelism. '*Believe* in it?', I retorted. 'I *rely* on it!' Evangelism is no longer seen as something under-taken only by cranks or well-meaning yet over-enthu-siastic college students; it is seen as integral to the life, mission and wellbeing of the churches. Evangelism is refreshingly *normal*!

This might seem to suggest that evangelism is just a pragmatic response to a situation in which it has become necessary. In fact, the current situation within the Western churches has led to the rediscovery, not the invention, of evangelism. In the 1890s, the Student Chris-tian Movement was founded. Its watchword was 'the evangelisation of the world in this generation'. Today, a century later, that vision is being rediscovered. Without realising it, Western Christianity had become dependent on the legacy of the Middle Ages in Europe. The idea of 'Christendom' had gained sway – that is, the idea of a defined geo-political area with a settled Christian world-view. Evangelism was unnecessary when Christian as-sumptions were so deeply rooted in society. But that situation has changed, especially recently, with wide-scale immigration into Europe from Islamic regions of the world, and the cultural erosion of faith by Marxism, relativism and other modern worldviews.

The new situation has prompted Christians to look into their past, and realise that evangelism was high on the agenda of the Church, until the rise of 'Christendom' made it unnecessary – in the apostolic Christianity of the New Testament itself, in the history of the early Church, and in the events of the 'Great Awakening' of the eight-eenth century. But we cannot rely on the legacy of Christendom any longer. Christianity must earn its position in society, not rely upon the past. Evangelism is the key to the future of Christianity in the West, as it stands poised to enter its third millennium.

We need to be clear about what evangelism is before we can move on to the main theme of this book – apologetics. The word 'evangelism' comes from the Greek word for 'gospel', and is probably best translated as 'proclaiming good news' or 'bearing good news'. At the heart of any understanding of evangelism are two ideas: first, the good news of Jesus Christ, which gladdens the hearts of men and women; and second, the need for this news to be proclaimed, if people are to hear and benefit from it. Note that the term has no overtones of manipulation, imperialism or authoritarianism. It simply speaks of the 'good news' of what God has done for weak, mortal and sinful human beings, and of the responsibility of those who have heard and benefited from this news to pass it on to others.

Evangelism rests upon the basic human desire to want to share the good things of life. We do not evangelise to score points off people, or to assert our superiority over them. If those motivations have been there in the past, then the Church needs to repent of them. The real reason for evangelism is *generosity* – the basic human desire to share something precious and satisfying with those who matter to us. It is like one beggar telling another where to find bread. It is an act of sharing, of refusing to keep something so wonderful and satisfying to ourselves. 'Taste and see that the Lord is good!', wrote the Psalmist (Psalm 34:8). If something really matters to you, you won't want to keep it to yourself!

An important part of evangelism is explaining why we are Christians. What is it about the Christian faith that matters to us? How does it make a difference to our lives? These sorts of things, simple though they are, can be of enormous importance in bearing witness to the presence and love of God in the world. At a more sophisticated

level, evangelism could be about presenting the full claims of the Christian faith, with an invitation to respond to them. But that could be a lot further down the line: we need to be sensitive to where people are. So important is this point that we need to take it further, by exploring what is meant by 'apologetics'.

Apologetics – A Cinderella Turned Princess

With the new emphasis on the faithful and effective presentation of the Christian faith, a neglected resource has come into its own. That resource is apologetics. Once a Cinderella, it has now claimed its rightful place at the royal ball. Everyone knows that jargon is a nuisance. Too often, it conceals the meaning of words, and allows professionals to hide behind a smokescreen of complex terms. 'Apologetics' runs the risk of falling into this category, yet the term can and must be used. It refers to a precise and well-defined area of Christian ministry which is related to evangelism, yet distinct from it. Apologetics is a kind of pre-evangelism, something that lays the ground for evangelism at a later stage. Let's explore how.

The Greek word *apologia* literally means 'a defence', or 'a reason for doing or believing something'. The word is used with this meaning at 1 Peter 3:15, where Christians are urged to 'give a reason [*apologia*] for the hope that lies within them'. Becoming a Christian does not mean kissing goodbye to rational thought. Apologetics is about giving reasons for faith. It is about persuading people that Christianity makes sense.

So how does apologetics relate to evangelism? A rough working definition of evangelism might be 'inviting someone to become a Christian'. Apologetics would then be 'clearing the ground for that invitation', so that it is more likely to receive a positive response. If evangelism is like offering someone bread, apologetics is about persuading people that there is bread on offer, and that it is good to eat. Apologetics stresses the reasonableness and attractiveness of the Christian faith; evangelism makes the offer of that faith.

A friend – whom we shall call Simon – had recently split up with his girlfriend, and was rather lonely and miserable. Feeling sorry for him, some female friends threw a dinner party for him. During the course of the evening, they talked about women, life, women, work and women. As they talked about one of their women friends – whom we shall call Jenny – they detected a noticeable quickening of interest on Simon's part. They extolled Jenny's virtues, and told Simon all about what she was like, and why they were so fond of her. He began to raise objections: perhaps she was already in love? Perhaps she wouldn't like him? They reassured him. Finally, they posed the crucial question: would he like to meet her? By then, he had decided that he would very much like to take this further. He agreed, and a meeting was set up.

Apologetics is just like the commending of Jenny to Simon. Positively, it sets out the attractiveness of the

Christian faith; negatively, it tries to neutralise some of the obstacles that come between people and faith in Christ. In the end, apologetics is about preparation – preparing the way for a relationship, whether that relationship is with Jenny, or with the living God.

This homespun analogy draws attention to a basic distinction between apologetics and evangelism, which is easily overlooked. Apologetics is non-confrontational. Evangelism is. It asks someone to consider whether he or she feels ready to take the step of faith – a step for which apologetics has prepared the way. To make this point clearer, we shall use the simple image of a road.

The Roads to Faith

Imagine someone setting out on a long and difficult journey, not quite sure where it is leading or how long it will take. Perhaps we could call this person a 'pilgrim'. Or we might use a Latin term that became popular in the Middle Ages: a *viator*, a 'traveller' or 'wayfarer'. It is an image that has captured the imagination of many novelists – most famously John Bunyan – who compare the human search for meaning in life to someone undertaking a journey. One of the most poignant of questions is, 'Where am I going?' because it is all too often asked by someone in despair, someone for whom life has little meaning, or who is contemplating ending it all. For there is something fundamentally restless and dissatisfied about human nature. People in secular Western society think more about the meaning of life than many Christians realise. Often a tragedy provokes this thinking, by challenging cosy and optimistic views about the human situation. The death of a close friend or relative can bring out the deep anxiety that most people have about death and dying. Not only have we lost someone who matters to us, we have also been reminded of the disturbing fact of our own mortality. Many people find that a deeply worrying thought, as they are conscious of having no answers or hope in the face of that event. Many novels and films express this deep feeling of anxiety and hopelessness in the face of death. True, they have no answers – but at least they make the problem crystal clear.

Some people outside the Church will have been impressed by the quality of the lifestyle of their Christian friends, and secretly wonder if they could share their hope in a good life after death. They may slip into church, quietly and unnoticed, to see if they could recover a faith which they allowed to lapse many years ago. Others may buy a Christian book, and read it in the privacy of their home. There may be obstacles of all kinds in their way. However, they have begun to turn their thoughts in a direction that they might have thought impossible in the past.

Each person has a personal road which leads to faith in Christ. For some, that road may be short and sweet; for others, it may be long and difficult, littered with obstacles. And, at the end of that road lies a decision – a decision to come to faith. It may be a decision which is taken easily, without undue effort. Some Christians have grown up in a Christian family, attended church regularly, and gradually come to accept and make their own the faith with which they have been surrounded since their youth. For others, the story is very different. As secularisation makes deeper inroads into Western society, it is becoming increasingly common for young people to grow up with little, if any, familiarity with Christianity. Their parents may have no faith of any kind. They may never have attended church. They may have learned nothing of Christianity from their school-days. So someone has to explain what Christianity is, and why it has exercised such an influence on the lives of so many men and women. Someone will have to listen to the difficulties and hesitations that these people will have. And, finally, someone will have to answer the

crucial question: what must I do to become a Christian?
The road may be longer; it may take a different form; but,
in the end, the result is the same. Someone moves to
faith. Apologetics aims to clear that road of obstacles to
faith. Evangelism provides the opportunity to respond to
the Christian gospel in faith.

To appreciate the importance of apologetics to the
tasks of the Christian Church, we may explore two
aspects of helping someone to become a Christian.

1. *Explaining what Christianity is all about.* In an
increasingly secular culture, fewer and fewer people
outside the Christian community have any real understanding of what Christians believe. Half-truths, misconceptions and caricatures abound. It is difficult for anyone
to get the straight facts. One of the most important tasks
of apologetics is simple explanation: nothing complicated – just a simple and clear presentation of the basic
elements of the gospel.

This doesn't require great skill or a degree in theology.
It isn't something that only professionals can do. It just
takes a little trouble. In one of his comedies, the French
playwright Molière tells of the man who spoke prose
without knowing he was doing so. Many Christians will
be surprised to discover that they have been doing
apologetics without realising it!

Perhaps you were hindered from coming to faith by
misunderstandings about the gospel. Try to remember
what they were. How did you feel about them? Did you
turn your back on a caricature of the real thing? There
will probably be people at your church who had very
muddled ideas about what Christianity involved. Listen
to them. Ask them to tell you about how they discovered
the truth, and the difference it made. It can be interesting, because you learn more about people, and discover
that they have depths which had previously been hidden.
And it can be profoundly useful. Someone may describe a

problem they had with Christianity, and how they resolved it – and, as you listen, you realise that someone close to you has that same difficulty right now. You listen more intently, in the knowledge that this person's experience could well be of real value to someone who matters to you.

2. *Helping people remove barriers to faith*. This is where apologetics comes into its own. Think again of each person's journey to faith as being like a road. That road begins where they are at present, and ends somewhere in the future, as they joyfully discover the wonder of the gospel. In between, there lies a series of barriers, each of which is like a roadblock to faith. For some, there may be many such barriers. For others, there may only be one. Apologetics aims to clear away those barriers.

Many Christians, however, are apprehensive about trying to deal with these barriers. What, they wonder, can they say that might be helpful to someone with such difficulties? They feel inadequate and useless. Yet many people often put their discovery of the gospel down to something that one of their Christian friends did or said, perhaps many years ago. Sometimes that person may have died without knowing that what they said or did would have such effect. We may never know the results of our witness. We need to learn to trust in a God who is able to take and use our feeble yet faithful efforts.

Some Christians get very discouraged. They want to be able to say things that will lead their friends and loved ones to faith immediately, and they are saddened and distressed when this doesn't happen. 'We have failed!', they cry. But it isn't that simple. They may well have removed one obstacle; yet others remain; but they will have left their friends one step closer to faith. We may not be able to bring people all the way to faith – but we can leave them closer to that faith than when we first met them. Someone else may have the privilege of removing the final barrier, and have the privilege of seeing a person discovering the joy of faith.

Starting Where People Are

One of the most important skills in apologetics is a simple willingness to listen to people. How far is a person along the road that leads to faith? And what are the obstacles that they are confronting? The only way to find out is to listen to people, and come to know them well. Try to work out where they are – and start from there. Some may be ready to make a decision for Christ; others may have a long way to go. Be patient! Try to avoid sounding like a tape recorder spewing out pre-programmed responses to pre-set questions.

The personal aspect of apologetics is of vital importance. The crucial question we need to ask is not, 'What kind of things stop people from coming to faith?' Rather, it is, 'What stops *this friend of mine* from coming to faith?' You may be the only person able to answer that question.

A friend of mine recently told me that she thought she would be lousy at evangelism. 'I'm basically a people-person,' she told me. By that, she meant that her basic concern was for people, rather than for ideas. I was delighted, and told her so. That's why she will be such a good evangelist. She cares about people, and takes trouble to get alongside them, to know them, and to care for them. In her life, she models God. How? By showing care, compassion, and commitment – just as God showed his love by sending Christ into the world to die for us. By meeting people where they are – just as God entered into this world in the person of Jesus Christ. And by showing how Christianity links up with people's heartfelt concerns – such as loneliness, fear of death, and worry about the future – she will allow those whom she loves to catch a glimpse of the love of God for them, and want to learn more about it. Evangelism takes place, subtly yet powerfully, every time we talk to our friends about our faith and hope, and try to share what it means for us to be Christians. We may not be able to find the right words, or handle all the objections and questions that are raised as we talk. But a powerful and lingering impression is created: individuals matter.

So take people and their problems seriously. Remember that your non-Christian friends may well judge Christianity by reference to you! That's a frightening thought! For them, you are Christianity embodied in a person. But remember that the love you show towards them reflects the love of God for his world. Remember that the seriousness with which you take your friends and their anxieties reflects the way in which God cares for them. You may not be very good with words or arguments. But your consideration and compassion may well help them to understand, appreciate and – finally! – respond to the love of God.

Apologetics, then, has two components, positive and negative. Positively, it is about identifying and setting out clearly the attractiveness of faith. And, negatively, it is about clearing away the obstacles on the road to faith. But what kind of obstacles? And how can we deal with them? Michael Green takes up the story.

2

Understanding Why People Are Not Christians

I was given a delightful video recently, called *It's No Good Shouting!* It emerged from a significant conference of thinking Christians on the gospel and our culture. It picked up, and refuted, characteristic English attitudes to foreigners who do not speak the language. If they don't understand, speak slower and shout louder!

This is, of course, as disastrous a way to approach those who do not share our faith as it is to those who do not speak our language. It is essential to try to understand why people are not Christians. Indeed, we shall

I SAID....

YOU REALLY NEED TO HEAR THE GOOD NEWS !!!

have little chance of seeing any change until we do. Gone are the days when we could simply preach the good news louder – and hope they would respond. They may not, for a variety of reasons. We shall look at four of the most common in this chapter.

Reasons of the Climate

In every generation, there is a dominant climate of opinion. And in Western lands, once so strongly influenced by Christianity, the climate of opinion is at best apathetic, at worst hostile towards the Christian faith. Why should this be? Why do we not have a flat playing field on which to play our game? For the answer, we shall have to delve, although briefly, into history.

If you had been around in Europe five hundred years ago, you would have lived in a society which was dominated by Christian associations – if not always by Christian faith and behaviour. For a thousand years, since the end of the Roman Empire, the prevailing worldview in Europe was Christian. The most beautiful buildings were Christian. The best art was Christian. Law and justice claimed to be Christian. International relationships operated, theoretically at least, within a Christian framework. The Church was the dominant force in society, the pope was more important than any prince. Thought itself was regulated by what the Church taught.

You might well be illiterate, but you would have seen God's handiwork in the fields where you worked each day, and heard his generosity to you in church on Sundays. The parish priest was, along with the squire, the most educated person in the village. You would have learned the catechism. You would imagine the world to be a three-decker universe – heaven above, the earth in the middle, and the underworld beneath. You would know many stories from the Scriptures and the lives of the saints. You would be well aware of the shortness of life; and the fear of death, and, worse, hell would often grip you. Much the same was true of North America in the seventeenth century, where the Church played a central role in the lives and thinking of the emerging nation.

Today, that climate has completely disappeared. We live in a society where Christianity seems to be a dwindling force, a minority interest. It seems to have lost any influence in the great cities where most people live. Art, literature and music are no longer concerned with religious themes. People are often extraordinarily

ignorant of the barest outlines of what Christianity is. There are no family prayers at home, no instruction in the schools. Few are confirmed, and those that are often have little idea of the catechism, and still less conviction of its truth or relevance.

Christianity seems to have nothing to do with relationships at home, in the market place, or in international relations. We are no longer illiterate – but few read the world's bestseller, the Bible. Churches are often deserted. Clergy are often seen as very odd fish. Nobody is quite sure what they are there for.

Our minds are anaesthetised to the pain which TV brings in ever increasing quantities into our homes. We feed those minds with magazines, game shows, soap operas, and thrillers. Death has replaced sex as the unmentionable subject. On the whole, for most people most of the time, the real world is so grim and the next world so unreal that we need escape routes which consume us – pop music, detective thrillers, TV sport, drugs and booze – if we are to survive our increasingly long and tedious life span. God never gets a look in.

The climate in Western Europe, North America and Australasia has become almost totally secularised. It is not that people have thought about Christianity and rejected it. It simply doesn't enter into their minds. By contrast, if you and I lived in Papua New Guinea, for example, we would find a totally different cultural climate. Everyone believes in God, and everyone believes in evil spirits. Evangelism is a very different matter out there!

What are the causes for this massive decline of Christianity in Europe, once the heartland of the Christian faith? A number of reasons may be given, each so powerful that they have combined to remove Christianity from the serious consideration of 90% of our population. The most important of these factors during the past five hundred years are probably the following:

1. *The rise of the European Renaissance during the fourteenth and fifteenth centuries.* A whole new world of learning was released, springing from the culture of classical Greece and Rome – its art, philosophy, science, and above all its humanism. Man, not God, became the measure of all things. This world, not the next, became the centre of attention. No longer was the Christian worldview the only one on offer: the seeds of both pluralism and secularism had been sown.

The Reformation in the sixteenth century brought a revolution in Church and society. The old ecclesiastical stranglehold was broken by the division of Christendom, and the dissemination of the Scriptures discredited much in contemporary Catholic teaching. The old 'priest' became the new 'presbyter'. The rise of the natural sciences, pioneered by men such as Copernicus and Galileo, liberated people from Church dogma and opened up a spirit of empirical discovery and hard work.

Meanwhile, nationalism was rearing its head. Devotion to the nation came to replace devotion to God. Europe was torn to pieces by war. This tendency has continued. The world is fragmenting into ever smaller entities when its overwhelming need is unity, after a half century which has seen a meteoric increase in weapons of mass destruction and has endured the two most terrible wars ever to have devastated the human race.

2. *The Enlightenment.* Headed by thinkers such as Descartes, Hume and Locke, the Enlightenment was an eighteenth-century development of Renaissance principles which has had an incalculable influence upon Western thought and attitudes. Agnostic about God, it wanted to place human reason in his place – a reason which would unveil a natural religion common to all of humanity, a universal morality in which everyone sought the greatest good of the greatest number, human rights were possessed by all people universally, society

was held together by a social contract (replacing the idea of the fatherhood of God and the brotherhood of man), and the universe resembled a great machine, intricate and self-sustaining.

The thinkers of the Enlightenment were for the most part optimists, and believed in the essential goodness of human nature and in the inevitability of human progress (which was given greater impetus by Darwin's theory of evolution). Although the Enlightenment was responsible for many benefits to humanity, there can be no doubt that its influence has, during the past two centuries, been a major factor in bringing about the common conviction that this world is what really matters, and that religion is at best empirically unverifiable and socially divisive.

3. *Scientific materialism and the associated technological revolution.* These have ushered us into a world utterly beyond the imagination of our forebears. Although it began in the Christian worldview of men who, like Bacon, believed that God had revealed himself in two books – the book of nature and the book of Scripture – science was soon seen to be independent of religious controversies, and capable of supporting a totally secular worldview. Married to Enlightenment rationalism and the principle of radical doubt, it rapidly became a serious threat to Christian teachings, as they were popularly perceived (though not necessarily to the gospel itself!).

Think of some of the fathers of science and the challenge which they presented to Christianity. Copernicus and Galileo, by recognising the nature of the solar system, challenged the Church's understanding of the earth as the centre of the universe. Newton's discovery of gravity challenged the commonly-held idea that divine providence maintained the planets in their courses. And when Newton's follower Laplace was rebuked by the Emperor Napoleon for having left God out of his scheme of the universe, he replied, 'Sire, I have no need of that hypothesis.' Darwin's theory of evolution was at once perceived to challenge the prevailing idea of God as creator.

These challenges have continued with Marx and Freud. Both these thinkers have had a decisive effect on the twentieth-century abandonment of God. Instead of Christianity's promised kingdom of God, Marx offered the idea of a class struggle eventually leading to economic and social Utopia. Freud undercut the whole Christian worldview by dubbing it, along with all religions, a purely psychological phenomenon. Is it any wonder that these varied streams of opposition to Christian belief and practice have brought about the climate of opinion in which we live today?

4. *Urbanisation.* This concentration of people into the cities of the world is one of the most powerful forces in our society. It has often had the effect of breaking family ties, uprooting traditional values, and alienating the mass of people from the rhythm of country life, which made belief in God very natural. This process of urbanisation is proceeding worldwide at a terrifying pace. Crime, the breakdown of relationships, alienation and unbelief in God are among its side effects. They are increasingly apparent in our societies.

These, then, are some of the reasons which account for the social and intellectual climate of our day. It is a climate which seems to make God an implausible hypothesis, a spent force. It helps us to see why many scientists, business people, psychiatrists, urban planners – in fact, almost everyone – feel that they can get along without God, if he exists, which seems rather doubtful.

The situation has not been helped by the Church's inadequate response to these developments. On almost every issue and occasion, it has hung on to its dogmas, and refused to face unwelcome new truths. Think of the fury of the Catholic Church against the Reformation. Think of its persecution of Galileo – for which the present pope has only now got round to making an apology, three hundred and fifty years late! Think of the disastrous nineteenth-century debate between Huxley and the Bishop of Oxford, which showed up the Church as the champion of obscurantism. Think of the way in which many of the churches have consistently opposed the quest for truth, the furtherance of human dignity, and the struggle for freedom and justice, which have been among the goals of the Enlightenment. During the Second World War, the Vatican seemed to be on the side of the Nazis. In Latin America it has been shamefully allied to ruthless ruling oligarchies.

As for the cities – the Church has never come to terms with the urban masses. Throughout Western society, the churches seem to abandon the city centres and move out to the cosy suburbs. It would be almost (though not entirely) true to say that the Church has habitually been reactionary. It has been seen to set its face against the causes of freedom, justice, inquiry and progress. It has done little to transcend nationalism, to understand the goals of science and democracy, and to reach the industrial workers of our great cities. In the light of this catalogue of past failures, is it any wonder that so many people are not Christians? If we are going to change the situation, we must begin by understanding it.

Reasons of the Memory

It is not only the climate of opinion which militates against a resurgence of Christian faith in the West today. I recall chatting with a Christian leader in Holland recently. He is pioneering a completely new type of church, because the memories associated with experiences in both the Catholic and Protestant Churches in that country are so unhelpful. And his warm, lively, relevant church (devoted to attractive outreach and emphasising every-member ministry) is having a great effect, not least in the red-light district of Amsterdam. Or I think of the open-air ministry which I used to attempt in Canada, when a normally quiet and friendly Canadian became abusive and even violent as he passed by and heard me speaking of God and the Church. It was because such talk stirred very painful memories. These people have been deeply wounded by institutional Christianity. They want to have nothing further to do with the Church.

Sometimes it is because of the heartless eviction of their family, when they were small children, from property owned by the Church.

Sometimes it is because of the banning from communion after divorce; the designation of marriage after divorce as living in sin; or the refusal to bury Dad in holy ground because he was an unbeliever.

Sometimes it is because a clergyman was reluctant to baptise a baby in the family where there was no evidence of any commitment to Christianity. Sometimes it was his insistence that the family should come to church for a few weeks before the baptism, or that the parents should attend a preparation class. Sometimes the chosen godparents were rejected because they did not seem to be practising Christians. The number of hurts and rebuffs, imagined or real, associated with baptism are enormous, and probably account for the drop in the number of infant baptisms in Britain to about 20% of the population when only decades ago it was virtually universal.

Sometimes the memory harbours resentment against the day when you were thrown out of the church youth club for a couple of weeks to cool your heels. Sometimes it was when the local pastor passed you by as if you didn't exist. Perhaps nobody from the church called to visit when Aunt Agatha was dying. Perhaps nobody even knew. No matter; it is a black mark against the local church, and you are not going to darken its doors again.

Sometimes the resentment is a result of marriage policy. What is all this about some clergy not being prepared to marry you unless you have been baptised? Or if you're pregnant? Or when they stop the photographers taking pictures in church? Or charge outrageous fees? Or subject you to dreary and uncalled-for marriage preparation? Many people's noses are put out of joint by the way they feel clergy have handled them at the most sensitive time of their lives, when a marriage was in the air.

Sometimes the resentment is against a particular person, who was a member of the church, and has hurt them deeply in the past. Or against some church official who swindled them in business – a manifest hypocrite. Sometimes . . .

The sources of resentment are endless. And there is a very good reason for this. Christians are human beings. All human beings are likely to make mistakes and are capable of deliberate wickedness. That is the point at which we are all equal. And those who hold resentments against the Church need to be shown that they too cause pain and provide stumbling blocks to other people. They need to learn the destructive effects of holding grudges. It simply breeds a cancer in the heart of the one who harbours it.

But the most common of all complaints against the Church can be summarised very succinctly: 'We were forced to go when we were young, and it was deadly dull.' Just think of that! Forced to go – why didn't the grown-ups go too, and make it a family affair, rather than something to be avoided the moment you grew out of short trousers? The answer is simple: the grown-ups did not believe or practise the Christian gospel, but still thought that Christian morals were a good thing (for the kids, anyway). So they sent them along to Sunday School to get some rough and ready ideas of right and wrong into their heads, while Mum and Dad had an extra hour

in bed on Sundays to read the paper. That is the escapism, the double standard, the hypocrisy even, underlying the 'sent to Sunday School' mentality. It is on the wane now. Parents neither go themselves nor send their children. But the institution of the Sunday School may have a lot to answer for. Under the pretext of instructing the young, it has separated families, and allowed people to think of themselves as Christian by proxy, while continuing to be totally untouched by the gospel of Christ to whose representatives they compel their young to go!

And think of the second part of that all-too-common complaint: 'We were forced to go when we were young, and it was deadly dull.' Deadly dull? How on earth do you make Jesus dull? The most blazing revolutionary that ever lived? The one who overturned attitudes to women and the outcast? The one who took on the religious and political establishment single-handed? The one who lived in poverty and endured with complete composure the most savage and unjustified attacks? The one who died a death of such love and self-sacrifice that

it has become the most famous death in history? The one
and only person in all the annals of human history to
have broken the grip of death? How on earth can you
make such a person dull? It is the most phenomenal
achievement of theological colleges, theological writers, clergy and Sunday School teachers that they have
managed the unthinkable – they have made Jesus dull.
And once people have got the idea that Jesus is dull it is
not easy to make them change their minds.

Reasons of the Intellect

Given the climate sketched in the first section of this
chapter, it is not surprising that many people in our
society have strong intellectual objections to the Christian faith. I do not think that this is the main cause of
contemporary unbelief, because (as Freud and Jung have
demonstrated) it is perfectly obvious that we are not
influenced by considerations of reason in all, or even
most, of our lives. Who gets married on the basis of
rational grounds alone? Yet although the mind is not the
most important gateway to the soul, it remains a very
important avenue. Any attempt to draw people to Christianity which evades the challenge posed to the human
mind by unbelief will not succeed for long, and does not
deserve to.

Donald Soper is one of the most celebrated British
popular apologists of today. Aged ninety, he still takes
on all-comers at Speakers' Corner in Hyde Park, London.
He knows the answers to many of the questions which
flood in. But most important of all – he knows all the
questions! I cannot lay claim to that, but I love debating
the faith with modern unbelievers. I have noticed that
the following nine arguments (all derived from the
amalgam of views which have gone to make up modern
scepticism) are brought forward more commonly than
any others. None of them is unanswerable.

1. The most basic objection is psychological: religion is a neurosis, and does not relate to anything real. This view goes back to Freud's *Future of an Illusion*, in which he predicted the early demise of religion in the light of his theories about the human ego. As it has turned out, religion has proved a lot more enduring than Freud's theories! It is demonstrably one of the most powerful forces, for good or ill, in the world today. It is a profoundly rooted human instinct.

Is religion the only human instinct which has no substantial basis? How are we to explain human society, the world in which we live, the laws of nature, the hunger of the heart, if there is no source greater than ourselves from which we come? To be sure, Freud thought religion neurotic; but that is arguably because he lived in an age in which Christianity was the prevailing background to society, and the sick people to whom he ministered had taken that background on board. He seems to have seen nothing of the manifestly non-neurotic and socially constructive activity which was going on in all parts of the world of his day, inspired by the gospel of Christ. In the end, Freud was forced to flee Vienna by jackbooted Nazi thugs who had swallowed the theory that religion was an illusion, and that might was right.

2. Another common objection is phenomenological in character; in other words, it derives from observing the world. It is impressed by the immense variety of beliefs sincerely held by pious practitioners all over the world. It concludes that there must be alternative or complementary routes up the mountain that leads to God and eternal life at the top. This is a warming liberal perspective. But, as we shall see in a later chapter, it is not one that will withstand too much critical examination. For one thing, this current variation on the doctrine of religious pluralism is not shared by the practitioners themselves. For another, there is no real agreement

about what the top of the mountain is, and whether or not there is any life to be enjoyed there! For another, the moral dimension of religion is totally ignored in this pluralist paradise: Satanists are placed on the same level as Mother Teresa. And – the most basic point of all – most of the people who favour this approach seem to know little about other faiths, or even any one faith! They just find pluralism a convenient way of ducking the commitment question. In any case, there are other parallels to consider rather than roads up a mountain. What about paths through a maze? There are lots of paths – but only one turns out to lead you safely through to the other side. The rest turn out to be dead ends.

3. Then again, we have logical objection. 'You can't prove that there is a God!' True enough. Neither can you prove that there isn't a God. The only way to logical proof would be to show that there is something greater than God, from which his existence could be deduced with certainty. But that is, by definition, impossible. After all, 'God' is the name that we give to the ultimate source of our world, beyond which it is impossible to go.

And if they ask (and they do love to!) 'Then who made God?' you can show them that this objection is also flawed. It would indeed be an infinite regress if God were just another cause or effect in a *finite* temporal chain – if he were what the philosophers call 'contingent'. But that is not what we are talking about when the name 'God' is used! We mean a self-existent being who is the source and origin of the world, as he is of the whole principle of cause and effect. There is no logical argument against an *infinite* personal source for ourselves and our universe.

As a matter of fact, there are very good reasons which point in that direction – for example, the fact that there is a world at all, or the fact of human personality, the fact of apparent design in our world at every level, the fact of human values, of conscience, and of religious belief. All these are undeniable phenomena, which point clearly in one direction – that there is some kind of God. You can't prove that there is a God, any more than you can prove that your mother loves you – but there is plenty of evidence to support the hypothesis!

4. A dying cry may still be heard, to this effect: 'We are all good people at heart.' Why is it dying? Because of the brutal and harsh facts of two world wars, and all the atrocities and suffering that they brought. Yet although it is dying, it remains vocal. 'There is no such thing as an evil person – just a socially deprived or psychologically imbalanced or sorely misunderstood person.' Many modern educational methods and some legal judgments have been based on that assumption. Yet it is manifestly false, and few people outside the senior common rooms of universities still hold to it. Humanists such as H. G. Wells, Bernard Shaw and C. E. M. Joad all held to this

idealistic view of human nature in their time – yet all had to abandon it in the face of the evidence to the contrary. There is something wicked in the human heart – in all human hearts – and it is unrealistic to deny it. Another and in some ways a parallel illusion is shared by Buddhism and Christian Science: evil is unreal. Try telling that to a man whose wife has been murdered and daughter raped! Christianity is thoroughly realistic about human nature.

5. There is a widespread conviction these days that truth is relative. You hear it when someone says, 'Well, it's true for me. I don't know about you.' In a world of so many conflicting ideas and cultures, it seems almost indecent to brand any statement or idea with the label 'true' or 'false'. Yet that is how it is, and that is what the words mean. We are perfectly happy to apply 'true' or 'false' to the public world of so-called facts – for example, that the Battle of Hastings took place in 1066, or the

BUT IT'S AN ABSOLUTE TRUTH THAT ALL TRUTH IS RELATIVE !!!?

Declaration of Independence was made in 1776, or that Wales beat England 10–9 at rugby football this afternoon. Yet we squirm when someone has the effrontery to apply the terms to values or ideas.

There is no need to cringe. There are important issues at stake here. Suppose your friend tells you that, 'All truth is relative; you must not make absolute claims for it.' The last thing that this friend will expect is for you to come back, and reply, 'That statement of yours is relative as well. It may seem OK to you, but it cuts no ice with me.' Although your friend has put forward the claim that all truth is relative, it is clear that he is making an *absolute* claim for that statement. Yet, on the basis of his premise, that is impossible! It makes no sense to say that it is absolutely true that all truth is relative. It will do your friends no harm to realise that they have been smuggling an unacknowledged absolute into a world which they claim to be totally relative!

6. One of the most common intellectual cop-outs you are likely to hear is that science has disproved religion: if you believe in science, you can't believe in God. A moment's thought will show that there is something seriously wrong with this objection. The most scientifically advanced nation in the world is the United States of America. It also happens to be one of the world's most openly Christian nations. In fact, this objection is a hangover from a nineteenth-century materialist worldview, which saw the world as a great clock. Now scientists see it more as a great mystery.

The feeling that science is opposed to Christian faith is probably also coloured by the depressingly bad attempts to defend the faith which Christians have made in the past in the face of scientific advances and truth-claims. Christianity comes across as defensive and reactionary – and nearly always wrong! But of course it needs to be remembered that natural science was born (and could only have been born) in a culture which valued honest inquiry and believed that no truth could harm you. That is an essentially Christian mindset. It is not surprising that many prominent scientists are deeply committed Christians, seeing no incompatibility between their trust in God as the source, sustainer and goal of the universe, and their strenuous and persistent inquiries into how it all works. By studying the creation, you come to learn more about the wonder of the creator! Science is the enemy of obscurantism, not Christianity!

7. Science, in showing the rational cause of so many things that were once thought to be inexplicable, has cast doubt on the idea of miracle. Now the word and the whole concept of 'miracle' need more careful definition and study than we have time for at this point. However, I do not see how you can be a Christian without belief in two miracles: the incarnation and resurrection of Jesus of Nazareth. It is totally against the normal run of experienced uniformities in our world for its creator to enter into it, within the womb of a virgin girl. And it is no less surprising and unprecedented for this same Jesus to be raised from the clutches of death after his very public and bloody execution.

This is the minimum claim that Christians can make for miracles. There is nothing irrational or superstitious about it. The claim is indeed *miraculum* – a 'wonder' – but it is attested by such a wealth of evidence, positive and negative, historical and circumstantial, that it is much harder to refute than to accept. We do not suppress our reason when we examine claims to the miraculous; we rightly use our reason to assess the strength of the evidence on which those claims are made. We also recognise that there is a power greater than our reason whose activities may well be beyond our intelligence, but will not run counter to it. On the basis of purely rational grounds, nobody is in any position to deny miracles. We need an openness of attitude and a careful, reasoned scrutiny in order to weigh up the truth claims presented.

8. A whole cluster of questions centre on the founder of Christianity himself. These are usually either historical or theological in nature.

The historical questions normally take forms such as the following: 'Did Jesus ever exist?' 'Was it all written down centuries later?' 'Can we trust the New Testament?' and 'Is there any unbiased reporting about Jesus?' Every pastor will have come across variations on these basic themes.

The answer is quite simple: not only did Jesus exist, but the whole of history has been dated from him. The questioner would love it to be the case that Jesus never existed, for then nobody need bother about him. But secular and Jewish, as well as Christian, authors attest his life and death and continued impact. It would be impossible to explain the rise of the Christian Church in the first century AD had Jesus never existed. His death was very public, and was noted by the Roman historian Tacitus.

And no, the evidence about Jesus is not late and unreliable. The gospels were not dreamed up in the second or third century. The textual tradition of the gospels is far stronger than for any other book in antiquity. The gap between the original text and our first extant copy is far shorter than for any other ancient book. The spread of translations and versions throughout antiquity makes it fruitless to doubt the integrity of the text. Copies of the text of all four gospels can be found as early as AD 160, while there is a fragment of John's gospel dating from even earlier, AD 100–125.

The gospels themselves have been subjected to a degree of scrutiny never applied to any other books before in history. They have emerged with their heads held high. Written between AD 60 and 90, their picture of

Jesus fits in brilliantly with that of St Paul, who wrote ten years or more before the earliest gospel. It is not the reliability of the New Testament which is at issue; it is whether we can face up to the challenge of the person displayed there. Scepticism arises not from the unreliability of the material, but from the stark challenge of the Jesus who meets us in its pages.

And what about unbiased reporting about Jesus? In fact, there is no such thing as 'unbiased reporting'. Everyone writes from a certain perspective. But there is certainly plenty of evidence for Jesus from sources which were biased *against* Jesus and his Church. The most well known and easily accessible are the references to Jesus in Tacitus *Annals* 15.44, Suetonius *Nero* 16 and *Claudius* 25, Josephus *Antiquities* 18.3, and Pliny *Epistles* 10.95, 96. These references, along with certain inscriptions and other archaeological finds, go a long way not only to giving independent attestation to the existence of Jesus, but also to presenting a picture of him which is very like that of the gospels.

The theological question about Jesus is simple. Was he just a great man, a wonderful teacher, a matchless guru? Or did he share the nature and being of God as no other person ever has, and is he therefore uniquely empowered to speak in his name?

This is not the place to go into the divinity of Christ. But the evidence is cumulative and persuasive. Moreover, it comes from people who were not at all predisposed to believe it. It was anathema to a Jew to suppose that any human being could embody the divine presence. Many Jews preferred to die rather than be made to worship the Roman emperor as divine. Yet many of the first Christians were drawn from these same Jews, who became convinced that Jesus was no less divine than he was human. You would not have found a more unpromising soil anywhere in the world in which to plant such an idea! Yet these intensely critical people were convinced

by a number of factors, all pointing in the same direction.

His *teaching* was more than merely human. Nobodyhad ever heard anything to touch it for profundity, clarity, breadth of appeal, and authority.

His *influence* was greater than that of any warrior, king or wise man. It touched all types of people. Had the evangelists lived a little longer, they would have seen it reach all nations.

His *behaviour* was impeccable. Nobody could throw mud at him and make it stick. He had all the virtues known to men and women, yet none of the vices. The ideal had lived in history.

His *fulfilment of prophecy* was unique. His conception, birthplace, teaching in parables, wisdom, salvation, triumphal entry into Jerusalem, his suffering, his ultimate vindication and victory after a shameful death, and his burial in a rich man's tomb – all these were predicted in Scripture centuries before. It all came to pass in this one man's life. That was unique.

His *miracles* powerfully attested his claims.

His *claims* – to forgive sins, to accept worship, to be the final judge of all – certainly persuaded his disciples. Their truth was self-evident.

Jesus' *death* clearly had an enormous impact on his followers. They saw it as something he did for the whole of humanity – something utterly without parallel.

And the *resurrection* of Jesus and his return to his heavenly Father, followed by the gift of his unseen Spirit which galvanised the infant Church into action – this was the foundation stone of their conviction that the Jesus whom they had walked with through the dusty fields of Palestine was the Lord of heaven and earth.

These evidences are just as powerful today. They point calmly and strongly to a Jesus who is no great teacher, no famous guru, no mere wonder worker, but the embodiment in human flesh of the living God.

9. The ninth objection to Christianity is something which all of us share in at some time or other – suffering. How, it is asked, could a good God, if he is as great as Christians say that he is, allow all that suffering in the world?

There is no knock-down answer to that objection in Christian theology, nor in any other worldview. Suffering is one of the ultimate mysteries of life for all of us, Christians and everyone else. But the Christian must not be embarrassed by the question. We have a better answer than anyone else! We will want to maintain that the loving and powerful God does indeed will our happiness and wholeness. But this is hindered by various factors, including human rebelliousness, which always involves suffering; the nature of the physical world, where pain is inevitable unless the laws of the universe are to be defied; the existence of a powerful force opposed to God, the devil, which is bent upon maximising pain and evil; and the interdependence of the cosmos and all who live in it.

We do not worship some cold and abstract God who set this world going with faceless laws, and then left it on its own. We are dealing with a God who suffers; a God who cares for us so much that he has intervened in person, and allowed the worst of human suffering to sweep over his person. He has personally shouldered its basic ingredient, human wickedness, through what he achieved on the cross. What is more, Jesus rose triumphant over suffering, sin and death – and that is pledge enough of the eternal destiny which awaits those who ally themselves to him. When it comes to the problem of pain, there is no anti-Christian objection which enables us more easily to relate the central message of the good news to a bleeding world.

Reasons of the Heart

We have looked, however briefly, at nine of the most common intellectual objections which people bring against the Christian position. None of them is ultimately compelling, although each of them has some initial appeal. Many people who make such objections often turn out not to have thought about them very much. They have rested content with their superficial understanding, until this is punctured by rigorous discussion. These people are comparatively easy to bring to Christian faith. Once you show them that their objection(s) are not sufficient to keep them from the loving arms of their creator and redeemer, they often take that step of commitment to him, and may become some of the most thoughtful and courageous Christian advocates in the Church.

But some who profess these very same objections are not doing so because they are genuine stumbling blocks in the path of faith. They are doing so in order to evade the challenge of faith. The situation is made more complicated by the fact that they may not realise that this is what they are doing.

But it remains true, as Pascal observed long ago, that 'the heart has its reasons'. Sometimes they are dark reasons. It may be some attitude, formed long ago, which Christian commitment would change. It may be some illicit relationship, long cherished, which obedience to the gospel might bring to an end. It may be some guilty secret, long hidden, which Christ would bring to light. In short, what seems to be an intellectual reason for rejecting the gospel may actually be a moral reason – not 'I can't believe', but 'I won't believe'. It is not a *reason* but an *excuse* for rejecting Christ.

This situation needs careful handling. If you answer a reason, it will smooth the way for genuine progress. If you answer an excuse, it will immediately be followed by another excuse! Great delicacy is needed. Often a comment like, 'You can't prove God' will turn out to be a genuine intellectual difficulty. Sometimes, however, it cloaks a deep-seated dread that the living God may invade my life and clean up the mess that he finds there. That would be a very painful experience. And so it is important that God is not real! I have found that one of the best ways of differentiating between a genuine difficulty and a moral smokescreen is to ask gently, 'Is this really the problem? If I could answer this to your satisfaction, would the way then be clear for you to entrust yourself to Jesus Christ and become one of his followers?' If the answer is 'No', then I decline to answer the question. You can't play games with the living God. Volition is as important as cognition in getting past these intellectual barriers.

Sometimes the reasons of the heart have a different cause. They are hurts inflicted on us by others in the past, and they inhibit our response to the gracious approach of Jesus.

Many people these days have a very low self-image. They have been made to feel that they are no good, that they will never make it. We have very good news indeed for such people. We can assure them on the most solid grounds that God values them so greatly that he came to earth to find them. He rates them so highly that he was prepared to die in order to win their love and allegiance.

Others – it would seem an increasing number – have been abused in their childhood and are overcome with shame. We have good news for them too – the Jesus who removes shame, whether real or imagined, in the warmth of his total and free acceptance, and then heals those deep wounds by the indwelling power of his Holy Spirit.

Others have never experienced love without strings attached. It has always been dependent on their performance and achievements. But the love showered upon us all by Jesus is unconditional. He knows the worst about us, but loves us just the same. Love like that can be a lifesaver to the earnest but unhappy achiever.

Others refuse to respond to the Christian offer because they know themselves to be defeated – defeated by habits which they cannot break, or by a lifestyle which they do not like, but are powerless to change. We have highly relevant good news for them, too. In Jesus of Nazareth they encounter one who can break every fetter and set them free. He is very experienced at it! He has been doing it all over the world for centuries.

It is as we approach such people with tender understanding and gentle explanation of that aspect of the gospel which speaks to their condition that they realise that Jesus is willing to take failures like them on board. Hope is born, and new life is begun.

3

The Art of Building Bridges

At the start of this book, we noted that apologetics has both negative and positive aspects. Negatively, apologetics understands and, where possible, neutralises the difficulties that prevent some people from coming to faith. The previous chapter explored some of these difficulties, and indicated how they can be overcome in sensitive and helpful ways. But there is also a positive aspect to apologetics – the identification and presentation of the attractiveness of Christianity. It is this which concerns us in the present chapter.

The Attractiveness of Christianity

As we have seen, a central task of apologetics is to make Christianity credible in the modern world. However, this is not easy in a pluralist culture where claims to possess 'the truth' are no longer seen as a positive. To declare that you believe in the truth is now seen by many people as arrogant and triumphalist, implying that everyone else is wrong. Truth-claims are often seen as a kind of intellectual fascism, as Allan Bloom pointed out forcibly in his influential book, *The Closing of the Modern American Mind* (Simon and Schuster). People who talk about 'truth' are seen to get in the way of an open society, which both recognises and takes delight in the variety of viewpoints on offer. At the academic level, this pluralist outlook finds its expression in postmodernism, with its vigorous rejection of universal truth claims and its commitment to openendedness.

So how can we cope with this development? Take the rise of the New Age movement, widely regarded by cultural analysts as a protest against the spiritual barrenness of the Enlightenment's emphasis upon pure reason. Many old-fashioned American apologists try to deal with New Age ideas by writing learned tomes, studded with footnotes, pointing out the logical and philosophical deficiencies of pantheism and panenthe-ism. And sure, there are problems with the religious outlooks of the New Age movement. The approach adopted by these apologists has the enormous advantage of intellectual sophistication and theological integrity. Nevertheless, it cuts no ice with the intended audience. It has strictly limited potential in public debate. It often casts the Christian apologist as boring, pedantic and petty, over against the openness of the New Ager.

For the argument is not taking place in university

seminar rooms, between pipe-smoking academics swapping stories about Kant and Hegel, but in the public arena – on television chat shows, in popular magazines, and supermarket checkout lines. And the vast majority of the public is not interested in conceptual sophistication and finely-honed technical arguments. It is interested in quickly-grasped and easily-understood points. And above all, it is interested in the bottom line: 'What's in it for me?'

We do not need to throw away Christianity's claims to truth in the light of this cultural development. We just need to realise that it's now bad tactics to major on the truth question, if it makes people think you are some kind of intellectual fascist. The situation demands that we rediscover the *attractiveness* of the gospel. This doesn't mean that we sideline the truth of the gospel, as if this doesn't matter. Rather, it means that we finally have to face up to the fact that, if we are going to get a hearing in today's culture, we need to be able to show that Christianity has something relevant and attractive to offer. The bonus is that this is securely grounded in God's self-revelation, not cooked up yesterday in an effort to get a hearing in the marketplace.

We may commend the attractiveness of Christianity, resting secure in the knowledge of its truth. The attractiveness of a belief is too often inversely proportional to its truth. The Christian, in enthusing about the attractiveness of the gospel and its enormous potential to transform human life, can rest assured that the gospel rests upon the bedrock of revealed truth, and that acceptance of the gospel glorifies God as well as transforming human life.

We do not need to *make* the gospel attractive, by dressing it up in modern clothes. For the gospel already *is* attractive. It is up to us to bring out this attraction as clearly as possible, and grounded in the situation of people we talk to. Above all, we need to take the trouble to relate the message to its audience, making sure that it scratches where people itch. The gospel proclamation must be 'receptor-orientated' – in other words, it must be addressed to individual needs and opportunities.

The Art of Building Bridges

The image of 'building bridges' suggests, first, the idea of bridging a chasm or gulf. Apologetics aims to build bridges between the Christian faith and the broader culture. It aims to make connections between the gospel and human experience – experience such as hope, fear, and joy. The task of apologetics is to show how the Christian faith is able to make sense of human experience.

Second, the image of building bridges suggests more than establishing contact; it points to individuals being able to cross a gulf, passing from unbelief or indifference to faith. Building bridges is about establishing contact with the non-Christian world, understanding it, and eventually providing a way in which people can cross to faith.

This might seem to suggest, however, that the task of building bridges is something we have to do – starting

from nothing. That would be an enormous task! However, the truth of the matter is much more exciting. God has already begun to build bridges for us. There are 'points of contact' for the Christian faith already in the world and in human culture. It is up to us to notice them, and make the most of them.

What sort of 'points of contact'? And how do they arise? The Christian doctrine of creation declares that God made us in his image and likeness, with an inbuilt ability to relate to him. Sin is fundamentally to do with the disruption of this relationship. Although we are created with the ability and intention to relate to God, this is frustrated through sin. As a result, we experience a sense of 'emptiness', which reflects an absence of God. As Blaise Pascal put it, there is a 'God-shaped gap' within us – a gap which really exists, and which nothing except the living God himself can fill. We have all watched children playing with a toy which involves placing pegs into holes. Only the square peg fits the square hole. And only God will fit this God-shaped gap.

This well-documented feeling of dissatisfaction is one of the most important points of contact for gospel proclamation. In the first place, that proclamation interprets this vague and unshaped feeling as a longing for God. And in the second, it offers to fulfil it.

In the first chapter of this book, we pointed out the importance of discovering and respecting individual needs. Good apologetics is person-based. It rests on knowing the needs, concerns and worries of individual people, and showing how the Christian gospel interlocks with those needs and anxieties. Good apologetics rests on two premises:

1. that you know something about your friends.
2. that you know something about Christianity.

The first poses relatively few problems for anyone; the

second may, in some cases, cause one or two difficulties. Far too many Christians know too little about Christianity! Both your friends and your Christian faith matter profoundly. Take time to get to know them both better!

One of the most exciting consequences of the new emphasis on evangelism within the churches is that it has encouraged Christians to find out more about their faith. It is much easier to explain something if you have thought about it yourself! A good understanding of Christianity can bring a new quality and depth to your discussions with your friends. But there is another benefit. I gave a lecture recently on 'Making Sense of the Cross' to a church group in Geneva, Switzerland. I pointed out how some of the ideas I was exploring would enable members of the audience to explain Christianity far more effectively to their friends. Someone came up to me afterwards. 'I don't know whether what you told us will help me evangelise my friends', he told me 'but it sure helped me to see things clearer!' One of the spin-offs of taking trouble to get to know more about Christianity is that our own faith is enriched and deepened as a result.

Let's look at an example to bring out this point. Take the meaning of the cross, the topic of those lectures in Switzerland. What is the cross of Christ all about? What did Christ achieve by dying on the cross? A basic understanding of the 'benefits of Christ' is of enormous assistance in trying to build bridges between the Christian faith and the lives and experiences of ordinary people. The death of Christ on the cross is enormously rich in its meaning, and includes the following five elements, each of which will have a particular attraction to different people.

1. *Losers turned winners*. Christ has gained a victory over sin, death and evil through his cross and resurrection. Through faith, believers may share in that victory, and claim it as their own. Many people are deeply anxious

about death, and find the thought of it unbearable. Christianity is able to interlock with this human feeling, and relate directly to it. The New Testament stresses that Christ died in order that we might be liberated from the fear of death (Hebrews 2:14–15). Socrates may have taught us to die with dignity; Jesus Christ makes it possible for us to die in hope.

2. *Forgiveness and more – righteousness.* Through his obedience on the cross, Christ has obtained forgiveness and pardon for sinners. Those who are guilty can be washed clean of their sin, and be justified in the sight of God, that is, acquitted of their sin and given the status of being righteous before God. Someone who is conscious of a deep sense of moral guilt, which prevents her from drawing near to God, will find the proclamation of forgiveness deeply attractive and meaningful. Knowing that her sins really can be forgiven could transform her life.

3. *Coming home to God.* As sinners, we are alienated from God. In the death of Christ, God was reconciling the world to himself, and he made a new relationship possible and available. Many people have a sense of 'being far from God'. Christianity declares that God has drawn close to them, and offers them the hand of friendship. Again, many people are conscious of having lapsed from a faith which they once possessed. They wonder if they could ever come back to that faith. Would God have them back? The parable of the prodigal son (Luke 15:11–32) makes it abundantly clear that God delights in the return of those who have sojourned in the 'far country' – wherever that may have been, and for however long it lasted. Like the waiting father, God is eagerly anticipating the return of his wandering children. A celebratory feast awaits them!

4. *True liberty.* Those who are imprisoned by the

oppressive forces of evil, sin and the fear of death can be liberated by the gospel of the cross of Christ. Just as Christ broke free from the prison of death, so believers can, by faith, break free from the bonds of sin, and come to life in all its fullness. A surprisingly large number of people sense that they are trapped in their situations – trapped by their own powerlessness, their enslavement to secret sins, or forces which lie beyond their control. The cross and resurrection of Christ offer the hope of liberation – and not only spiritual liberation. There have been many remarkable spin-offs of evangelistic ministry in the United States and the Far East. One of them is that some people hooked on narcotics find they can finally kick the habit on conversion to Christianity.

5. *Healing and wholeness.* Those who are ill on account of sin can be made whole again through the ministrations of the wounded physician of Calvary. Through his cross and resurrection, Christ is able to bind up our wounds and heal us, restoring us to wholeness and spiritual health. Opponents of Christianity often point out how the churches attract many of the weaker and more hopeless members of society. So they do. And why? Because these people appreciate that Christianity has something to offer them – something which nobody else seems able to offer. The Church has been compared to a hospital (see page 82) – a group of people who need healing, and are finding it in the midst of a loving and caring community.

Notice that this approach does not reduce the cross to a single idea. Instead, it aims to identify the different ideas and images that are already there in the gospel message. One or more of these may prove to be of decisive importance or attractiveness to someone who is hearing the gospel for the first time. But this does not mean that the message of the cross has been *reduced* to that theme. It simply means that we take trouble to find out what our resources are, so that we can connect up as effectively as possible with the needs of the individuals to whom we are ministering.

So how does this work out? Let's suppose that you are talking to a friend. Perhaps you have just been to a colleague's funeral together, or have been discussing how widespead AIDS has become. As you talk, you realise that she is frightened of dying. It would be entirely appropriate for you to explain why death doesn't frighten you as much as it once did. You would not be imposing upon your friend, or exploiting her, any more than if you were to offer her an aspirin for a headache, or tell her about a book you enjoyed reading recently. You would explain how your faith enabled you to cope with the thought of death. You don't need to ask her to share your faith. In effect, you are telling her something about yourself, and something about Christianity, at one and the same time. (In our secular culture, surprisingly few people know why Christians celebrate Easter; this conversation would thus be educationally useful!) By picking up the great theme of resurrection and hope, you are helping her to understand more about Christianity. The long-term outcome may be that she will decide to make this faith her own.

Does that mean reducing the gospel to the hope of eternal life? No. It is to recognise that this is a point of contact for the gospel for this person. The rest will follow, as the implications of the healing brought by the gospel begin to dawn in her new life of faith. The component of the message of the cross which addresses this fear of death is like the thin end of a wedge – it secures a point of entry. It is an emphasis within the message, not a reduction of the message to a single point. And, as many discover, the best wine of the gospel is sometimes kept to the end. The aspect of the gospel which attracts someone to faith is often overshadowed in later Christian life, as another aspect of the gospel

comes to be understood, and its attraction appreciated fully.

We cannot leave the gospel proclamation unfocused and generalised, on a kind of 'to whom it may concern' basis. The gospel concerns individual people and situations; our job is to make those connections, grounding the gospel in the specifics and particularities of those we talk to. We must be prepared to identify the attraction of the gospel for others, and make its attraction for us visible in our lives. The worshipping church community is, and ought to be, one of the most important forums of evangelism, as Christians express, in music and praise, their love of and delight in their God. As survey after survey demonstrates, most people do not come to faith through logical arguments or rational proofs for faith. They are drawn on account of the obvious attraction of the gospel for those whom they love, and a deep-rooted feeling that they themselves lack something important. Apologetics has got to learn to take these considerations into account. Otherwise, it will get nowhere – fast.

But how can ordinary Christians make sure that they do justice to their faith? We owe it to ourselves and to

God to explain the Christian faith for all its worth. The following four suggestions may well prove useful.

1. *Read some books.* A later section of this book identifies books that are likely to be helpful as you try to follow through some ideas and issues of potential importance. But books are not just of use to you! You can lend them – perhaps even give them – to your friends, in the hope that they may prove helpful.

2. *Listen to sermons* on key issues of relevance to apologetics and evangelism. If your local clergy don't preach on these themes, ask them to do so. It is an area of major importance to the future of the Christian Church, and clergy are under an obligation to be of every assistance to the people under their care. They can always invite in visiting preachers. If all else fails, use the tape libraries of churches which have longstanding preaching ministries in these areas. Most big cities have churches where the regular preaching diet includes coverage of these key issues. Make use of it!

3. *Join study groups.* Many local churches run study groups which provide a forum for discussion of these issues. Try calling your local church office for details. If there isn't one, think about establishing one, perhaps with the assistance and guidance of some friends. You can discuss books or other materials of relevance to these issues. You could share your experiences of trying to communicate the Christian faith in the everyday world.

4. *Attend conferences* on these themes. Many centres throughout the Western world offer regular courses, study days or summer schools on the themes of this book. Ask to be put on their mailing lists. Many Christian seminaries lay on extension courses for the benefit

of those wishing to increase their understanding of Christianity, while holding down a full-time job. Write for details. And remember that attending these courses will do far more than educate you. It will introduce you to other like-minded people, allow you to hear the top people in the field speaking live on the issues of the moment, and give you the chance to put your questions and raise your special concerns in plenary sessions or workshops.

A section at the end of this book provides information on all these matters, and will allow you to take these things further, if it seems appropriate.

Our attention now shifts to specific groups of people to whom bridges need to be built.

4

Building Bridges to . . .

As we have just seen, good apologetics is about relating
the gospel to specific needs and situations. This chapter
aims to provide some guidance about how to relate the
gospel to different types of people. It will be obvious that
each section is more a series of hints than an exhaustive
treatment of the subject in question!

Apathetic Materialists

Apathy rules OK! Or so it seems, as we cast our eyes over
modern Western society, where any interest in the
spiritual side of life is overshadowed, if not eclipsed, by
a preoccupation with things material. But a deep sense
of unease has descended upon many hitherto apathetic
materialists, who have up to now been cushioned from
some of the harsher facts of life through the economic
prosperity and 'feel good factor' of the 1980s. The myth
that materialism satisfies now seems to many to have
been publicly discredited. Marxism, perhaps the only
ideology to promote a purely materialist worldview,
has died in front of our eyes.

In the midst of this loss of faith in materialism, the
Christian can gain a renewed hearing for the gospel.
There are still many apathetic materialists around us;
but there are also many disenchanted materialists,

surveying the wreckage of careers and visions, and wondering if they could find something which is more satisfying and enduring. Materialism is deeply vulnerable at the moment – a window of opportunity which those concerned for Christian renewal must make the most of. It is perhaps no accident that periods of growth in the Church often seem to be linked with economic decline. The proclamation of the gospel today meets with a sympathy which would have been unimaginable at the height of the economic boom of less than a decade ago. Is it an accident that the Decade of Evangelism coincides with a period of economic depression? Or may we see the hand of God's good providence, preparing the hearts and minds of hitherto apathetic materialists to learn of the bread of life which endures and satisfies, when material prosperity and business confidence seem to be failing?

In what follows, I want to identify one 'point of contact', through which Christians can gain a sympathetic hearing for the gospel. This is *a sense of emptiness or dissatisfaction.* Awareness of such a sense of emptiness resonates throughout secular culture. One thinks of Boris Becker, the noted tennis player, who came close to taking his own life through being overwhelmed by this sense of hopelessness and emptiness. Even though he was enormously successful, something was missing. 'I had won Wimbledon twice before, once as the youngest player. I was rich. I had all the material possessions I needed: money, cars, women, everything . . . I know that this is a cliché. It's the old song of the movie and pop stars who commit suicide. They have everything, and yet they are so unhappy . . . I had no inner peace.' Or one thinks of Jack Higgins, a highly successful thriller writer at the top of his profession, author of bestselling novels such as *The Eagle has Landed.* He is reported as having once been asked what he now knew that he would like to have known when he was a boy. 'That when you get to the top, there's nothing there,' was his reported reply.

Becker and Higgins are excellent witnesses from the world of secular culture to this vital point of contact with even the most hardened 'apathetic materialists'. Most people are aware that something is missing from their lives, even if they may not be able to put a name to it or do anything about it.

It is this kind of feeling which underlies the famous words of Augustine of Hippo, an early Christian writer: 'You have made us for yourself, and our hearts are restless until they rest in you.' The Christian doctrines of creation and redemption combine to interpret this sense of dissatisfaction as a loss – a loss of fellowship with God – which can be restored.

This sense of dissatisfaction is explored further by the Oxford don C. S. Lewis. Lewis discovered Christianity (much to his surprise!) towards the middle of his life, and devoted the rest of it to writing and speaking about the coherence and credibility of faith. Although Lewis is best known for his Narnia books, such as *The Lion, the Witch and the Wardrobe*, he was also one of the most widely read and respected apologists of the modern period. Lewis wrote of 'a desire which no natural happiness will satisfy', 'a desire, still wandering and uncertain of its object and still largely unable to see that object in the direction where it really lies'.

Lewis points out that there is something self-defeating about human desire. Why? Because when we achieve the things that we long for, they somehow seem to leave us unsatisfied. The paradox of hedonism – the simple fact that pleasure cannot satisfy, so that the pursuit of pleasure is ultimately self-defeating – is a good example of this curious phenomenon. Even in our contentment, we still feel the need for something which is missing, but whose absence seems only too acute. There is a 'divine dissatisfaction' within human experience. This naturally prompts us to ask whether there is anything which may satisfy the human quest to fulfil the desires of the empty heart.

Lewis declares that there is. Hunger, he suggests, is an excellent example of a human sensation which corresponds to a real physical need. This need points to the existence of food by which it may be met. Any human longing, he argues, points to a genuine human need, which in turn points to a real object corresponding to that need. And so, Lewis suggests, it is reasonable to suggest that the deep human sense of infinite yearning which cannot be satisfied by any physical or finite object or person is a real human need which points to its fulfilment: in God himself.

Here, then, is a God-given point of entry for the gospel. We can talk to people about our faith, knowing that beneath the confident or apathetic exterior of our materialist neighbour there may well lurk a deeply unhappy person, who is looking for a pearl of great price, for the bread of life – that is, for something that is worth having, and that satisfies. So let us commend the deep sense of satisfaction and fulfilment that the gospel brings to our lives, in the knowledge that some, overhearing our comments, will begin to consider the claims of the Saviour who is able to bring such richness and joy to this poor and hope-starved world!

High School and University Students

College students are one of the most important categories of people to whom bridges need to be built. The great nineteenth-century Cambridge preacher Charles Simeon knew this. Whenever an undergraduate came into his church, he would say to himself: 'There's another six hundred people!' In terms of their future influence, they can be of immense importance. Today's college student is tomorrow's social, political and religious leader. Students are also often very open to considering the Christian faith at this stage in their lives. All of us engaged in student ministry of any kind know how exciting and demanding it can be.

So how do we build bridges to students? I write as one who discovered Christianity as a student. Maybe my own experience might be helpful to others! I went up to Oxford University in 1971, as a committed atheist. Like many young people of the time, I had been deeply influenced by Marxism, and had rejected Christianity as the 'opiate of the people'. I was capable of standing on my own two feet; I didn't need this kind of crutch to support me. In any case, Christianity was just a means of delaying the revolution. Such views were very fashionable in those days. But, if I was being entirely honest, I think I would have to admit that I had rejected a caricature of Christianity, rather than the real thing.

On arriving at Oxford, I met some Christian students. Like many people of my age (I was eighteen at this stage), I was determined to keep an open mind about things. I decided to give Christianity another chance. And gradually, I noticed things. I noticed that my Christian friends had a quality of life that I envied. I also went to some Christian meetings, and discovered that Christianity did not seem to say the things I thought it did. In fact, it said a lot of things that made sense. Gradually, I came to the point where I decided that I wanted to accept Christianity, and make it my own.

Now that's not a very interesting story (although it matters a lot to me!). Nevertheless, it does illustrate some important points. First, many college students do have open minds. They may well have rejected Christianity in their youth. Increasingly, however, social trends mean that many young people know nothing about Christianity at all. As a result, they have not been disillusioned by it or prejudiced against it as a result of over-enthusiastic Christian schooling (how many people have been turned off Christianity for life by compulsory school chapel?). Nor have they reacted against Christianity as part of the adolescent programme of rebelling against parental authority. All that has changed.

Once, Christianity represented the establishment against which it was *de rigeur* to rebel. Now, that same gospel is often seen as an exciting new cause, something to discover as part of growing up independent of parental constraints. I've met many American college students who have become Christians, whose parents were baby-boomer hippies. While working among students in Australia, I was deeply impressed by the number of students who were the first Christians in their families in living memory; they had come in from the cold entirely on their own, without any parental support or influence.

So the first point is simple. Explaining what Christianity is all about can be news to lots of young people. We cannot take it for granted that they will have rejected Christianity; they may not even know what it is. One of the best forms of apologetics is the clear and patient explanation of what Christianity really is, and what its attractions are. Very often, there is no need to defend the Christian faith – there are no prejudices to defend it against!

A second point concerns the public image of Christianity in schools and colleges. Students are often concerned about how they are perceived by their fellow students. To be a Christian is often to be seen as a freak. Sadly, it must be recognised that in part, this image is fostered and nourished by those in positions of influence within the educational establishment. Let me explain what I have in mind.

I grew up during the 1960s. It was a fascinating time to be young. It seemed as if a new age was about to dawn. In the United States, the civil rights movement blossomed, there were mass protests against the Vietnam war, and tens of thousands packed into the tiny town of Woodstock to hear the music of the coming generation. In Paris, students rioted, protesting against the establishment. Something new and irresistible seemed to be about to happen. And it was generally agreed that the future held no place for religion. John Lennon asked us to imagine a 'world without religion – a sort of paradise on earth.

In the end, it all came to nothing. Religion has made a powerful comeback, and is widely recognized as one of the most potent factors in modern international politics. But many who grew up in the 1960s cherished the vision of a world without religion. *And many of them are today in senior positions in high schools and universities.* The result? High school and university students are often put under the authority of men and women who have a deep-rooted hostility towards any religion. One recent survey suggested that 30% of American college professors had no religious commitment of any kind. This means that students are vulnerable. They need help and support, if their faith is to survive in such a negative environment. Religion is all too often presented to them as something which is outdated and discredited. And that puts Christian students on the defensive – against their teachers and against their peers. I have seen the same pattern in the problems faced by university students in the United States and Australia, by high school students in the United Kingdom, and international school students in Switzerland. It is tough being a Christian on campus.

Yet there is much that can be done. For example, students are often reassured when they see that intelligent and approachable people can be Christians as well. The work of national and international student Christian organisations – such as Campus Crusade, Inter-Varsity (IV) in North America, the University and Colleges Christian Fellowship (UCCF) in the United Kingdom, the Australian Fellowship of Evangelical Students (AFES) – is of vital importance. They are able to encourage students, provide fellowship for them, and above all to set before them credible and encouraging role models – that is, people with high credibility in student circles, who have no hesitation in affirming and

proclaiming their faith. The reinforcement of a positive image for Christianity in high school and university is of central importance apologetically.

A third point in bridge-building to students also concerns the public image of Christianity. Many non-Christians still think that, for example, Christian worship is all about little old ladies listening to an old man dressed in black speaking old-fashioned English to the accompaniment of deadly dull sixteenth-century music. Sadly, that still remains the popular stereotype of Christian praise! Could anything be more alienating to young people? Happily, this perception can easily be changed – simply by inviting such sceptics to a service at a lively local church catering especially for young people. Their prejudices may well be swept away in the first blast of heavy rock, harnessed to the proclamation of the good news of Jesus Christ.

A fourth point relates to the specific needs of young people. Western society is fragmenting, often causing considerable emotional damage to college students from broken homes, with permanently absent fathers. One of the most powerful bridges that can be built to college

students is friendship. This simple fact will appal some
people. 'Surely apologetics is all about arguments!', some
will complain. Now arguments have their proper place.
However, one of the most effective arguments for a
loving God is not philosophising about the problem of
suffering; it is simply showing love, care and compassion
to others. Young people need to be loved, accepted and
cared for. And in our behaving in that way towards them,
we are opening a window through which the love of God
may be seen. Building personal bridges to college students is of major importance.

In helping college students to understand and appreciate the Christian faith, it is important to bear in mind
two anxieties which trouble some of them. First, some
students worry about the long-term future of Christianity. They are young; they want to be sure that they are
committing themselves to something that will still be
around and relevant in their old age! This is understand-
able. After all, many of my student contemporaries back
in the 1970s were Marxists. I haven't met one of them
since then who retains that worldview. Might not Christianity go the same way?

There are several very important things that need to
be said here. Marxism is a human invention, a political
philosophy which reflects the social situation in Germany of the 1830s. No wonder it has proved utterly
incapable of relating to the global situation of the
1990s! Christianity is a universal faith, dealing with the
universal human predicament of sin and mortality. But
more than that: Marxism is a system someone invented.
Christianity is a response to a loving and living God. As
Paul reminded the Christians at Corinth (1 Corinthians
2:1–5), their faith did not rest on human wisdom, but on
the power of God. We are not dealing with some throw-
away package, but with something that is here until
kingdom come! This is where older Christians have a
real role to play. They are able to demonstrate that

Christianity has long-term potential, simply by virtue of their being – and continuing to be! – Christians.

The second difficulty concerns saving face. Although this is probably an issue for many people thinking about becoming Christians, it is especially acute for college students. Their public image matters to them! Becoming a Christian often results in public humiliation. So how can we be of use here? The insight of the Harvard Negotiation Project may be of help. Based at Harvard University, and developed by leading academics such as Roger Fisher, Willison Professor of Law, this project has concentrated upon ways of resolving difficulties without losing face or compromising personal integrity. There are two basic principles which should be applied:

1. *Separate the problem from the people.* Why do people get locked into an argument? Because they feel that their personal integrity is totally dependent on not admitting that they are wrong! To become a Christian amounts to admitting that they are wrong – which leads to a shocking loss of face. The basic strategy is as simple as it is effective: separate the people from the ideas. Help the other person to see that there is not necessarily a connection between their personal identities and the ideas they hold at the moment.

Does this mean that we are using unacceptable means of explaining the gospel? Are we using highly pressurised sales methods to put people under an obligation to accept the gospel? Certainly not. It simply means taking the trouble to work out why people have difficulties in accepting the gospel. Anyway, we aren't trying to sell anything – we're trying to give something away.

2. *Make it easy for them to change their minds.* People find it difficult to change their minds, if they are made to feel it is a win or lose situation. Bad apologetics creates the impression that changing your mind is equivalent to

losing an argument. And nobody likes losing arguments
– especially in public. Roger Fisher and William Ury,
explaining how the principles of the Harvard Negotiation Project may be applied, make this point as follows:

> Often in a negotiation people will continue to hold out
> not because the proposal on the table is inherently
> unacceptable, but simply because they want to avoid
> the feeling or the appearance of backing down to the
> other side. If the substance can be phrased or concep-
> tualized differently so that it seems a fair outcome,
> they will then accept it ... Face-saving involves
> reconciling an agreement with principle and with the
> self-image of the negotiators. Its importance should
> not be underestimated.

So how can this basic principle be applied? Two major
strategies are useful here. First, do not force your
conversation partner to enter into a win or lose situation. The simplest way of doing this is the following. Do
not present Christianity as being *right* (which immediately implies that your conversation partner is *wrong*,
and thus provokes a confrontation). Instead, present
Christianity as being *attractive*, explaining why. Chris-

tianity gives you hope in the face of death, a sense of peace in the presence of God, a new perception of personal dignity, and a revitalised sense of purpose (to name but a few of the many attractions of the gospel).

What perception does this create on the part of your dialogue partner? That you are concerned to offer him something which you have found valuable and exciting. You are not telling him that he is wrong; you are offering him something of value. The negative impression you avoid creating is that of defeating your colleague in an argument. The positive impression you succeed in creating is that of caring for your colleague. And is this not one of the fundamental impulses underlying all good apologetics – a sense of love and compassion for our friends?

Second, use yourself as an example of someone whose mind has changed. Clearly, this approach depends upon your having once been a non-Christian, and subsequently changed your mind. If this is the case, you can help whoever you are talking with to see that their personal identity and their ideas are separable. You could say something like this: 'I used to think that Christianity was something of an irrelevance. But I had the courage to change my mind. And I'm glad I did.' Acknowledge the problem, indicate that facing and resolving it is a matter of courage, and emphasise that the outcome of that decision was positive. The instinct to 'save face' is thus outweighed by the greater human instinct – to do something courageous, and which is *seen* to be courageous. Little things often matter a lot in apologetics; too often, they get overlooked.

New Agers

One of the most important alternative belief systems in modern Western society is loosely known as the 'New Age movement'. This media-generated catch-all phrase embraces a whole range of late twentieth-century spiritual practices and beliefs, especially on the west coast of the United States. In many ways, the New Age movement is a natural reaction to the efforts of a generation of pseudo-intellectual liberal Protestant writers and preachers, who attempted to get rid of the supernatural, mystical, and transcendent element from Christianity because 'people don't believe in these any more'. People got bored with the resulting liberal religion of platitudes, and embraced the New Age instead.

The New Age movement stresses the common identity of the human and the divine self. To use a phrase strongly defended by many New Agers: every human being is a god. Shirley MacLaine, publicly defending this key New Age doctrine in New York, was challenged by one of her audience: 'With all due respect, I don't think you are a god.' Her immediate response? 'If you don't seen me as God, it's because you don't see yourself as God.'

The attraction of this idea is enormous. If you are a god, you can make your own rules, and nobody can argue with you. Laying down the law is, after all, one of the privileges of divinity. Unlike Christianity, there are no 'Ten Commandments' or 'Sermon on the Mount' to provide moral guidance; the New Ager can rely upon 'the god within' to provide a conveniently undemanding ethic of self-fulfilment. (Interestingly, many New Agers profess to admire the religious teachings of certain Hindu gurus, but are less than enthusiastic about the rigorous programmes of abstinence linked with these teachings.)

New Agers are reluctant to put a name to God: to define is to limit, and God is limitless. Your mind gets in the way of knowing God. Stop using it. Don't evaluate. Don't judge. Don't think. Just allow yourself to *experience* God. There is no way of validating this experience. Just let it happen; what happens to you is God. You are

God; your experiences are thus divine. Deep within this approach lurks an obvious – some would say, fatal – contradiction. As G. K. Chesterton pointed out, worshipping the 'god within' turns out to be nothing more than self-worship. And if we are all gods, why is there so much misery in the world? Are gods unhappy creatures, condemned to a life of misery? New Agers seem to be just as unhappy as everyone else!

Now these ideas are not new. Indeed, one of the curious things about the 'New Age' is that it seems to rest on some very old ideas. The paganism of late antiquity has been revived, merged with ideas drawn from native American religions, and supplemented by pantheistic ideas deriving from Eastern religions. The revival of pagan ideas has reached such proportions that modern Christians can relate with great ease to New Testament accounts of Christian encounters with classical paganism (such as Paul's famous 'Areopagus Sermon', Acts 17:19–34). The New Testament includes a number of models of how to build bridges to paganism; we can make use of these in our own day, as we try to connect up with people involved in the New Age.

Let's note a problem relating to apologetics before going any further. As we have seen, the New Age does not have well-defined doctrines of God, generally believing that to define God is to limit him. It is perhaps more appropriate to speak of the movement having themes or attitudes, rather than definitely shaped belief systems. This feature of the New Age movement is perhaps one of its most frustrating features; open to endless variations, the movement cannot be defined with any degree of precision. What approaches may be adopted in responding to it?

The sort of simple and unsophisticated arguments that are likely to get home to New Age devotees are pragmatic and direct. If you are a god, why are you so unhappy? Why do New Agers suffer, like everyone else?

What's special about them? What privileges does being a
god confer? Does it make them immune from unemploy-
ment? From suffering or pain? From death? What hope
does it offer?

In the end, the debate with the New Age movement will
not be won through philosophy, but through the proclamation of Christ. The New Testament offers us invaluable
guidance here, which we ought to feel confident about
accepting. Paul's Areopagus sermon sets before us a
crisp, concise and convincing approach, ideally suited
to the New Age challenge – both in terms of the movement's ideas, and the opportunities available for confronting it. As for the Athenians the resurrection of
Christ may hold the key to engagement with New Agers.

Consider near-death experiences, often cited by New
Agers as evidence both of the reality of the supernatural,
and of their own interpretation of the realm of 'transcendent knowing, a domain not limited to time and
space'. These accounts are related by those who are

thought to have come very close to death, yet survive to relate what they experienced. But none of these reports concern experiences of *death*, or of *what exists after death*. They are simply perceptions of what seems to happen *close* to death.

But what if someone were actually to die and return from the dead to tell us about the experience of death, and what lies beyond? Would not his witness be of first-rate importance? Would it not possess an authority totally lacking in any other? Would we not pay attention to such a person? The Christian has immediately gained a hearing for Christ, and the message of the gospel – in terms that make sense to New Agers. It may lack theological sophistication. It would cut little ice in a philosophy seminar. But so what? We have to learn to adapt arguments and imagery to suit our audience. Learn to gain credibility in terms of the worldview of the New Age. Otherwise, you won't get a hearing.

You may wish to take a more sophisticated approach. Consider New Ager Marilyn Ferguson's words: 'You have to be willing to have experiences and not have words for them.' But why? Why not be able to put one's experiences of God into words? If God is so wonderful, he should be talked about. Why should God be nameless and thus unknown? Christ puts a name and a face to this God; the resurrection establishes his credentials in this respect. To lapse into quasi-New Age language, Christ has broken through into the realm of transcendent knowing, making it knowable and available. Such an approach – also used by Paul at the Areopagus (see Acts 17:24–28) – provides a point of contact, in that it builds bridges to the New Age, without endorsing it, in order to establish the authority of Christ – the resurrection being of supreme importance. The authority of Christ having been established, the apologist is in a position to begin introducing other key aspects of the gospel proclamation to his or her audience.

A third approach might be to argue along the following lines. The resurrection shows that Christ has some superiority over the rest of us when it comes to knowing spiritual reality. So we should listen to him, as one who has penetrated far deeper into the transcendent realm of knowing than anyone else. Again, note the emphasis upon the resurrection. Christ has a spiritual authority, which sets him above others. Why listen to Shirley MacLaine, when you can listen to Jesus? Jesus's credentials are more impressive than hers! Shirley hasn't died, let alone been raised from the dead, and thus hasn't had a first-hand account of transcendent spiritual realities. By operating tactically within a New Age worldview, you have set the scene for presenting the Christian gospel, eventually allowing your audience to break free from their existing worldview. You have built bridges to the New Age, by taking its adherents seriously. That simple care and concern may help them to move away from its ideas.

Wounded Religionists

There is nothing like a negative experience of religion to keep agnosticism in business. I had very negative experiences of Christianity from my own schooldays at a very religious boarding school in Northern Ireland. By the end of my time there, I was a convinced atheist. Yet, as I look back on those days, it seems to me that my youthful atheism was not actually the result of any real intellectual difficulties with Christianity. I was simply nauseated with compulsory chapel services. I was looking for faith; what I was forced to accept was religion. It was hardly surprising that I rejected it!

Many people are outside the churches precisely because they had such bad experiences inside them! In an

earlier chapter, Michael Green noted some of the powerful 'reasons of the memory' which dispose people against
Christianity. So how can we build bridges to them?

In the first place, we need to be honest: Christianity
has acquired a bad odour for many people, with some
justification. Some Christian churches are insensitive to
people's needs. Many Christians find their faith faltering
on account of the arrogance of a pastor, the thoughtless-
ness of other members of the congregation, or the appal-
ling public image presented by some publicity-seeking
Church leaders. At the same time, it needs to be pointed
out that Christ came to call sinners. Augustine of Hippo,
an early Christian writer, likened the Church to a
hospital – an institution full of wounded people, who
badly need healing. Christians are sinners: forgiven
sinners, sinners who are trying to mend their ways by
the grace of God, but sinners nonetheless. They make
mistakes, and they need forgiveness. Try to explain to
your friends that they must not judge the gospel by its
weak and fallible human representatives. After all, think
how much worse they might be if they were not Christians!

In the second place, explain the difference between
faith and religion. Faith is a trusting human response to
the love of God. Religion is a human invention, something that human beings have constructed. Religion is
all too often about outward observance of ritual and
external appearances. Faith, on the other hand, is about
our turning to God in trust and joy. It does not involve
any rituals; just accepting thankfully all that God offers.

'I can't stand religious people!' a friend once told me.
Your friends have probably been turned off Christianity
by religion. Try to help them discover faith! Point out
how the New Testament, and especially the teaching of
Jesus, is refreshingly free of religious stipulations! For
some people, discovering the distinction between 'religion' and 'faith' is one of the most liberating things that

ever happened to them! Help them to discover the love of God, and discard oppressive and petty human rituals.

But there remains a further category of people. This is a group who have become involved with Christianity in one of its high-pressure forms, usually of an evangelical or charismatic variety. They have found the emotional demands it makes too much to cope with. They have suffered from burn-out, and have been left reeling from their experiences.

These people need space to recover, and freedom to lick their wounds. The last thing that they need is to be placed under any kind of pressure. Help them to talk about their experiences; try to understand how they feel about them. The more relaxed and less demanding atmosphere of most mainstream churches may provide them with exactly the climate they need to recover, and begin to rebuild their faith.

Other Religions

Western society is becoming increasingly multicultural. This means that building bridges to people of other faiths is becoming of increasing importance. So how can this be done? In the space available, it is impossible to give detailed advice concerning the many non-Christian religions that you are likely to come across. The bibliography provided at the end of this work directs you to resources which you will find helpful in the case of the specific religion you are dealing with. However, the following general principles are helpful.

First, people of other religions will probably share with Christians a concern for the spiritual side of life. They are likely to be as critical of the typical Western obsession with materialism as Christians are. This is vitally important, as it establishes significant common ground.

Second, remember that there is considerable respect

for Jesus Christ amongst members of other religions –
especially Muslims. A discussion of major importance
can centre upon the question 'Who is Jesus, and why is
he so important?' Be prepared to talk about the resurrection! What actually happened on Easter Day? What does
it tell us about the identity of Jesus? And what's in it for
us? This immediately shifts the discussion away from the
rather vague idea of 'Christianity and other religions',
and focuses it directly upon a question of history – what
happened to Jesus?

Third, appreciate that many non-Christians have
negative feelings about Christianity, for historical reasons. Some Muslims, for example, still feel intensely
resentful against Christianity, on account of the crusades of the Middle Ages. They view the crusades as an
attempt by Christians to impose their faith on countries
of the Middle East. It is important – and entirely correct
– to disown these past events. Christianity was not
meant to be spread at the point of a sword. It commends
itself on account of its intrinsic merits, truth and
attractiveness.

Fourth, be aware of a deep fear of many people – that
becoming a Christian means bidding farewell to their
own cultures, including many of their most cherished
features. Thomas Aquinas, one of the most important
Christian writers of the Middle Ages, spoke of 'grace
perfecting, not abolishing, nature'. By this he meant that
the gospel brings things to perfection. It does not destroy
or deny what is good; it allows that goodness to be
brought to its fulfilment. At its best, Christianity seeks
to honour and preserve what is good in other religions –
such as the genuine search for truth, and a passionate
quest for true knowledge of God. The manner in which
Christianity relates to the Old Testament law is an
excellent example of this point. Christ declared that he
had not come to abolish that law, but to fulfil it – in other
words, to bring it to its intended perfection. People who

come to Christian faith from other religious backgrounds often speak of a sense of joy or delight at discovering how they can retain many of their finest and deepest hopes, through realising that these reach their climax and fulfilment in Christ.

Finally, the very act of showing friendship to people of other religions is in itself a vitally important witness. It mirrors the love and care of God for all his people. By taking the trouble to relate to such people, we are conveying the message that there are no barriers to the saving love of God. Failure to do so might be taken to suggest that God does not care for them, or that they lie outside the sphere of his grace. Personal friendships always matter – but especially in this context.

But another issue needs to be raised here – perhaps the biggest issue of all relating to other religions. How can Christianity make truth claims in a modern Western society which is so obviously pluralist in character? Michael Green takes up the story.

5

Christian Confidence in an Age of Pluralism

All Western countries are 'plural' societies these days. Many races, faiths and cultures go to make up the texture of the land. Immigrants from Europe, Africa and Asia form a growing proportion of our population and together they help to shape our culture and share in our common life.

But this neutral and very evident fact of *plurality* must be distinguished from *pluralism*, in the sense in which it will be used in this chapter. Pluralism is a prevalent and pervasive ideology which has swept through much of our society and has greatly influenced Christian thought. It distinguishes between facts and values. Facts are public: we are all expected to agree with them. There are scientific facts like the boiling point of water and historical facts like the Battle of Waterloo. Facts are public, and agreed.

But it is very different with values and beliefs. They are extremely diverse. There is no publicly accepted norm. In the area of beliefs and values pluralism rules. You have your views: I have mine. It does not matter, so long as we do not inhibit each other's freedom to express our private values and follow our private beliefs. None of them is absolute. None of them should be taught as 'truth' like facts. They are all relative. And in matters

of religion, certainty is impossible and would in any case be undesirable because it would prove socially divisive. All religions lead to God. Sincerity, not truth, is the supremely important thing. Tolerance is what matters.

That, then, is our modern situation. On facts we must all agree. On beliefs we agree to differ. In a climate like that it is very difficult to take a stand for the uniqueness of Jesus Christ, as the Way, the Truth and the Life. To make such a claim is one of the fastest ways to win the reputation for being narrow, intolerant and fanatical. It will attract opprobrium not only from atheists, agnostics, and adherents of other faiths, but often from Church representatives as well – who all, in their creeds and liturgies, profess to believe in one God and one Saviour of the world, Jesus Christ!

What has happened to account for this yawning chasm between what the churches profess to believe and what many of them actually believe?

We shall examine the root causes of the change below, but it is very evident that the current 'political correctness' makes two assumptions. One, that we all know what we mean by 'God' and 'religion', though in fact both are very slippery concepts. And second, that all religions lead to God, just as all spokes of a wheel lead to the hub.

That is thought to be the only enlightened view that tolerant people can hold in what has become a global village. And if it conflicts with some of the more dogmatic claims of Christianity, that is too bad: they must be dropped or reinterpreted. It is happening all the time. Jesus is now seen as either a great charismatic religious

leader – among others: or else he is seen as the embodiment of some abstract ideal – guru, freedom fighter or
'man for others'. In neither case can we – or should we –
swallow the time-honoured but untenable dogma of
Jesus being God incarnate.

Views like that are very common. What are we to make
of them? This chapter will take us into rather more detail
than some of the others because pluralism is both complex and widespread.

Pluralism is Not New

It is often suggested that twentieth-century thought has
made historic Christianity untenable. We form part of a
generation that has now become too sophisticated to
believe orthodox Christianity any more. But this view is
mistaken. It is not the discoveries of the twentieth
century that have led to pluralism, but rather the
collapse of Enlightenment views which have held the
intellectual stage for two centuries and more. In the
heady days of Descartes, Locke and Hume there was a
cheerful ditching of the notion of divine revelation, and
a deep confidence in the power of reason to provide
foundations for our truth claims. But it has not happened. The goal of finding universal truths in a universal
morality based on reason alone has proved illusory.
There are no absolutes in ethics or philosophy to which
reason can point with certainty. And the crisis in modern
thought is not due to some suddenly discovered flaw in
Christianity but to the breakdown of that rationalistic
worldview. Pluralism expresses secular human despair
at finding any universals. So all viewpoints are up for
grabs: you simply take your pick.

But it would be quite wrong to suppose that pluralism
is new. It did not originate in the late twentieth century,
though the current climate in our secular society is
particularly suited to it. No, pluralism has always been

an option. It was there in Abraham's day. The Old Testament is the story of the people of Israel attempting to stand up for the one true, holy God who saves, in the face of immense religious pluralism all round them – from the Caananites, the Moabites, the Egyptians, the Assyrians, the Babylonians, the Zoroastrians and the Romans. The people of Israel needed no lessons in the phenomenon of pluralism. They knew all about it at first hand – and they weren't having any of it. As the Romans found out to their amazement, Israel was passionately monotheist and would die rather than allow the merest shadow of polytheism to infect their holy land. And die they did in their hundreds of thousands throughout the various uprisings when the country was under direct Roman rule. Opposition to pluralism was an essential article of their faith. There was one true God – and no runners up.

It was precisely the same with the first Christians. Their message was of one God who had revealed himself decisively in Jesus the Messiah, one way of cleansing for human sins and frailties, one kingdom of love and loyalty to God into which all nations were invited, one way of acceptance depending not on religious pedigree or moral achievement but on the sheer generosity of God – all this they maintained with fearless courage in the face of a religious pluralism that makes our version look mild. Naturally they were unpopular. Yet had they adopted one of the 'correct' religious attitudes, the early Christians would have been left undisturbed by the Roman authorities. For the Romans were very broad-minded in matters of religion. When they conquered your territory they tended either, like the Hindus, to add your special deity to the existing pantheon, or else to identify him, as modern pluralists would, with a deity of their own who fulfilled roughly the same function. It was only when the first Christians stood out, and refused the twin expedients of addition and identification that all hell broke loose in vilification and spasmodic persecution.

So let us not buy into the idea that pluralism is a new problem, and that the proper Christian response is to go along with it. It is not new. And we are not to succumb to it. Visser t'Hooft, the first Secretary of the World Council of Churches, rightly observed, 'It is high time Christians should rediscover that Jesus Christ did not come to make a contribution to the religious storehouse of mankind, but that in him God reconciled the world to himself.'

Pluralism has a Growing Appeal

Though far from new, as we have seen, pluralism undoubtedly has a large and growing appeal in the modern cultural climate. There are historical roots for this.

One lies, obviously enough, in the widespread influence of the Enlightenment. If, for all practical purposes, you eliminate God, as Enlightenment thinkers did, how are you to evaluate rival religious claims? Without revelation, how can you choose between them? A pluralist attitude is called for.

The other lies in the Romantic movement which had a large following in the early nineteenth century. An important thinker who was influenced by this movement was Friedrich Schleiermacher. Acutely sensitive to the possibility of historical or scientific assaults on the faith, Schleiermacher maintained that the essence of Christianity was not the self-revelation of the transcendent God who had acted and spoken in Jesus Christ. No, the essence of Christianity and all other religions lies within 'God-consciousness'. The inner world of feelings and intuition, the sense of awareness of God – this was something that neither history nor science could disprove. He thought he was defending Christianity, as did Rudolf Bultmann a century and a half later: but both were in fact undermining its foundations. Schleiermacher believed in Christianity not because it was final or authoritative – its doctrines were all negotiable – but because Jesus had experienced that 'God-consciousness' in a completely pure form, and had offered some approximation of that to his followers. But the rot had set in. 'Let no one offer the seekers a system making exclusive claims to truth,' he said, 'but let each man offer his characteristic, individual presentation.' Such a view leads directly to late twentieth-century talk about experiencing the divine in a variety of ways, through the world spirit, the life force, reality and the like. On this view Christianity has no special claim to truth. Jesus is different in degree not in essence from any other great teacher. Calvary provides one way to salvation, to be sure; but there are plenty of others. The Scriptures, like other holy books, are purely human documents with many good and true thoughts about divinity and morality in them. And all religions lead to God.

And these twin influences of the Enlightenment and Romanticism are clear to see in the work of modern theologians. Hans Küng sees salvation being on offer to men and women through whatever religion and culture they happen to have been born in. John Hick talks about 'global religious vision' and a spirituality which is totally relativist. Ralph Waldo Emerson cries: 'Man is weak if he looks outside himself for help. It is only when he throws himself unhesitatingly on the God within him that he learns his own power.' That might have been written not by a Christian theologian but by Shirley MacLaine. It is pure New Age thinking, and it fits in not only with the New Age but with traditional atheism. There is no God out there, up there, beyond our world, to whom we can turn and from whom we can expect an answer to our prayers. As we have seen in the last chapter, the path is not up there or out there but *in*

there: the trip within leads to the only divinity there is, and you find it in the recesses of your own being.

It is instructive to note the development of this essential unbelief, even though it is often clothed in religious terminology. A vague, holistic vision has taken the place not only of the distinction between God and man, as taught by orthodox Christianity, but even between the duality of man and nature, as taught by the Enlightenment. Now we are encouraged to see man and nature as different dimensions of a single cosmic unity. But as C. S. Lewis perceived long ago, once you lose sight of a transcendent, personal, holy God, you are on a stopping train to pantheism. And that is where pluralists like John Hick, Jack Spong, Paul Knitter and their colleagues are inescapably headed. Don Cupitt has already – and avowedly – arrived there.

I do not for a moment want to deny that sort of outlook is very attractive. We have a new global consciousness these days. The confrontation of the superpowers is a thing of the past. The survival of the race depends on racial harmony and co-operation. But we do not need to deny our Christianity, in order to engage in the pursuit of peace and co-operation among nations!

We also have a new understanding of other faiths these days. People from all over the world jostle in our streets. There are more Muslims than Baptists in Britain, for example, and many of them are very highly motivated to win recruits. But what truth is there in Islam or Hinduism or Sikhism which is worthy of universal application, but which you cannot find in the life and teaching and enabling of Jesus of Nazareth?

We have a new embarrassment about colonialism in mission these days. After World War Two the colonial period died away, and with it the notion of white superiority. And so it should! The evangelisation which took place during the colonial period *did* get mixed up with business exploitation and Victorian attitudes which have nothing to do with the gospel. We can only repent of those things, but we have no cause to repent of fulfilling the Master's call to go and make disciples of all nations. Many of the Christians in Third World countries thank God for the missionary movement which brought the gospel to them and delivered them from bondage to animistic powers. There is an important distinction between the gospel of Christ and the cultural package in which it is received and passed on. It is not easy to disentangle the two, but every country and every generation must seek to test culture in the light of the gospel – whether that culture be national or Western. It is highly significant that the gospel is growing fastest in those parts of the world which might have had cause to complain of a colonial Christianity!

These, then, are some of the reasons for the growing appeal of pluralism, matched as they are by the decline of zeal, Bible reading, and churchgoing in Western Europe, as well as the diminished influence of Christian standards on culture and legislation. A post-Christian West is in no condition to resist pluralism.

Pluralism Will Not Do

Christians ought not to fear pluralism, though unfortunately many do. We feel we dare not advance our convictions for fear of embarrassing or hurting others. So we stay silent. Or perhaps we feel that we will get shot down in flames by the adherent of some other religion of which we know little or nothing.

But such fears should not haunt us. Pluralism is very much in the air, and that gives us, along with others, every right to be heard. There is no reason why we should not humbly but confidently speak of Christ, as our forebears did, and let the truth prevail. Of course we do so in a world where many views are on offer: there is nothing new in that. Of course we do so in a world where many cultures coexist: but there is nothing new in that, either. The Christian gospel has always been proclaimed against such a background. What is new is the claim that all viewpoints are equally valid, so long as they are sincerely held, the claim that the real danger is the person who believes in truth. Such a person is thought to be a sort of intellectual fascist! But that does not follow in the least. We are called to bear witness to the gospel, and let the truth prevail. After all, if Christianity is not true, we shall not want to have anything to do with it. If it is an illusion, we shall not want to credit it. But if it is the truth of God we need have no embarrassment in putting it before one and all for their consideration, saying, as it were, 'I am interested only in the truth, as I hope you are. Try this for size.'

We should not fear pluralism, then, but we should have no truck with it either, for a number of reasons.

1. *Pluralism makes some very strange assumptions.* One is that to affirm the truth of Christianity belittles other faiths. It seems arrogant and triumphalist to claim to have found the truth. It puts others down. Not at all! If you are truly Christian you respect all human beings, created as they are in the image of the God who created you. You revel in all things that are true in their

convictions. You listen to see whether their insights may correct your own understanding of the good news. But you do not need to abdicate your convictions to do so. Respect for others, even flat-earthists, does not mean that you have to agree with them.

Another assumption is that because there are so many religious views in the world they ought all to be regarded as equally valid. There is a deep-seated fallacy here, which philosophers have noticed down the ages: the attempt to deduce what ought to be from what is. There is a diversity in religious faiths: that says nothing about whether that ought to be the basis on which we evaluate them all. And it certainly does nothing to suggest that none of them may be right.

Another assumption is that all religions lead to God. That sounds wonderfully liberal, but it is nonsense all the same. How can all religions lead to God when some of them do not believe in a personal God at all, like Buddhism, while others believe in many gods, as in animism? Some believe in an inscrutable deity who cares nothing about the world he set in progress, while others maintain that God is personal, loving, intensely concerned with us, and has come to rescue us from our predicament of alienation from him and from each other. The whole idea of 'God' is different in these contrasting viewpoints. The notion that all religions lead to 'God' is ludicrous.

That point may be granted, but your liberal pluralist may respond, 'These admittedly different faiths have a common core to them. We need to restate "God" as "ultimate reality". Naturally, people's perception of that reality will be determined by the country and the culture in which they were born.' That sounds reasonable, until you ask whether the 'ultimate reality' of Satanism is the same as the ultimate reality of the Father of Jesus. In any case, it is an untenable view. It would make truth dependent on the country of your

birth! If I had been born in Russia and brought up as a Communist, would that make Communism true? If I had been born in ancient Rome I would probably have been a polytheist. Would that make it true? Moreover, this liberal dogma makes no allowance for the remarkable phenomenon of people from all over the world coming to see that their culture pointed them to the fuller light revealed in Christ. It stumbles on the rock of conversion – and about 70,000 of those take place every day, mostly in countries in the Two Thirds World where Christianity is emphatically not the religion in which people were born and raised.

Another assumption that underlies pluralism is that in the last analysis, sincerity is all you need. Believe it sincerely, and you will be fine. But this is so self-evidently crazy that nobody would attempt to apply it to any other area of life. I may sincerely believe that a bottle of whisky a day is good for me, and act on it, but that will not prevent cirrhosis of the liver. Sincerity is no guarantee of truth. We can be sincere and wrong.

These are very insecure foundations for modern Western liberals to advance a doctrine of pluralism, and I see no good reason to follow them.

2. *Pluralism is based on an outdated liberalism.* One of the great attractions of liberalism is its rejection of dogmatism and its appeal to human experience. It is very attractive to suppose that in our global village all religions are basically much the same, and their adherents experience more-or-less the same things. But that is an entirely unjustified assumption, and it is not borne out by the religious experience to which liberals appeal. A Muslim fundamentalist zealously killing Christians in Northern Nigeria may not be having at all the same religious experience as the animist seeking to buy off the evil spirits, or the Hindu guru meditating on reality. If you ask converts from other faiths they will tell you, as they tell me, that their experience is totally different from what it was in their pre-Christian days. I think of one Indian, nurtured in Hinduism, who is now an Anglican priest. He told me that he profoundly valued his cultural heritage, but that nowhere in Hinduism did he have any concept of God as Father, personally and intimately concerned for him. And nowhere did he hear of any way of dealing with the wickedness within him, for which he has now found a medicine in the atoning cross and risen power of Jesus. Try telling him his 'religious experience' is just the same in Christianity as it was in Hinduism: it is profoundly unconvincing! Indeed, this liberal view that all religions bring you into touch with the same reality, and share a common core, is not as objective as is claimed. 'Why should we accept a liberal interpretative standpoint, which owes little if anything to Christian beliefs, and is only "objective" in the minds of those who espouse it? *All* vantage points are committed, in some way or other. There is no neutral Archimedean point' (Alister McGrath).

He goes on to draw attention to an even more serious consideration. The liberal worldview is on the way out. Though so dominant in the 60s and 70s (and still among theological professors reared during that era), liberalism is as dated as the Enlightenment of which it is the offspring. A new school of interpretation is on the way up, called 'postliberalism'. It rejects both the Enlightenment appeal to 'universal reality' and the liberal assumption of a 'common core of religious experience' underlying all religions. Instead, it emphasises the importance of history in shaping the values and faith of a community. Now, postliberalism will not be the last word in theology! But at least it is a move in the right direction, and a warning against being taken in too much by a 'politically correct' liberalism which has already been on the wane since the 1980s. If Christian churches attach their approach to other faiths to a dated worldview that all religions are basically the same, they will discover the truth of Dean Inge's famous dictum, 'He who marries the spirit of the age today will be a widower tomorrow.'

3. *Pluralism displays a disturbing arrogance.* Despite its emphasis upon openness to other viewpoints, liberalism is actually profoundly dogmatic and arrogant. It is right, and others are wrong. Professor John Macquarrie makes the point with characteristic clarity:

> What is meant by liberal theology? If it only means that the theologian to whom the adjective is applied has an openness to other points of view, then liberal theologians are found in all schools of thought. But if 'liberal' becomes itself a party label, then it usually turns out to be extremely illiberal.

It does in this instance. Pluralists tend to pour scorn and even hatred on traditional Christian beliefs. John Hick denounces 'exclusive' approaches to religions as 'wrong' (whereas on his presuppositions he should only declare them as having a different perspective). He calls the traditional 'salvation through Christ alone' statements of the 1960 Congress on World Mission 'ridiculous'. Rosemary Radford Ruether thunders, 'The idea that Christianity, or even the biblical faiths, have a monopoly on religious truth is an outrageous and absurd religious chauvinism.' There is a lot more intemperate language of that sort in the pluralist collection *The Myth of Christian Uniqueness* (SCM Press). The pluralists show themselves to be open to anything except biblical Christianity. It may sound very liberated to maintain that there is a 'God behind God' to which all religions point and in which all religious experience shares. But this very soon becomes a liberal form of fundamentalism. They will join hands with all from whatever faith who hold this pluralist view, but will rubbish and ridicule Christians who hold to Scripture and to Christian orthodoxy.

And that seems to me to betray a double arrogance. It seems arrogant of Christian theologians to imagine that they know better than the Jesus they profess to serve. He took his stand unwaveringly on the divine revelation of the Old Testament. How do they airily wave away the authority to which their Master held so firmly?

It seems arrogant, also, to pay no attention to what the real adherents of other faiths say. Ask a Muslim in the Persian Gulf if he thinks all religions are different roads to the same goal, and your life may be in danger. I do not exaggerate. I simply wish to point out that it is not the different religions but the Western pluralists who cling so rigidly to this dogma that all religions have a common core and are fundamentally the same. They have succumbed to the very absolutism which their theory was invented to avoid.

Lesslie Newbigin makes this point with his usual perceptiveness. He refers to the story, beloved by pluralists, of the blind men and the elephant:

The real point of the story is constantly overlooked. The story is told from the point of view of the king and his courtiers, who are not blind, but can see that the blind men are unable to grasp the full reality of the elephant and are only able to get hold of part of it. The story is told constantly in order to neutralise the affirmations of the great religions, to suggest that they learn humility and recognise that none of them has more than one aspect of the truth. But, of course, the real point of the story is exactly the opposite. If the king were also blind, there would be no story. The story is told by the king, and it is the immensely arrogant claim of one who sees the whole full truth, which all the world's religions are only groping after. It embodies the claim to know the full reality which relativizes all the claims of the religions.

You see, it is only the king who is able to bring together the apparently unrelated experiences of the blind men who are each feeling some bit of the elephant. And the king who sees all this turns out to be none other than the Western pluralist!

4. *Pluralism is morally defective.* It does not have anything to offer us in our moral dilemmas. It is both ethically irresponsible and morally impotent. Why?

The God we worship will determine, to a large degree, the way we act. Worship a cruel God or an evil God, and your lifestyle will show it. To claim that it does not much matter which religion we adhere to is in effect to say that it does not much matter what behaviour we adopt. The two are integrally connected. And that is very evident today when decline in religion in Western countries is accompanied by massive moral collapse. Relativism in belief and relativism in morals go together. The result is disastrous. Think of the unwanted girl children left exposed to die on the hillsides of ancient Greece. Think of the human sacrifices to the fish deity in ancient

Polynesian religion. Think of the murder and gang rape carried out by practitioners of Satanism. Are we to believe that these all spring from differing insights into the same ultimate reality, as the pluralists claim?

Not only is pluralism ethically irresponsible: it is also morally impotent. It gives you no ethical standard, and offers you no moral power. It is implacably opposed to the life-transforming experience which Christians call conversion and the new birth. Such opposition is tragic. For the gospel of Christ makes tremendous moral transformations all over the world. Charles Darwin was so impressed by the changes brought about through the missionary work in Tierra del Fuego that he became an associate member of the South American Missionary Society! History is studded with the lives of men and women from every religious background, and from none, who have found in Jesus Christ a moral power that brought them an undreamed-of liberty. This happens to societies as well as to individuals. Think, for example, of the Sawi tribespeople in Indonesia, savage cannibals and ruthless killers, for whom treachery was the highest virtue. Through the courageous and imaginative evangelism of Don Richardson, whole villages of these people were won to Christ and their way of life utterly transformed for the better. There is no such life-changing power in the 'least common denominator' approach of pluralism. Well did C. S. Lewis observe,

> The God of whom no dogmas are believed is a mere shadow. He will not produce the fear of the Lord, in which wisdom begins, and will therefore not produce the love in which it is consummated. There is in this minimal religion nothing that can convince, convert, or console. There is nothing therefore which can restore vitality to our civilisation. It is not costly enough. It can never control or even rival our natural sloth and greed.

5. *Pluralism is allergic to the question of truth.* The great danger, as the pluralists see it, is not error but intolerance. Openness, tolerance is the only virtue in fashion today. It is the great insight of our times, and as Allan Bloom has put it so sharply in *The Closing of the American Mind*, 'The true believer is the real danger. The study of history and of culture teaches that all the world was made in the past; men always thought they were right, and that led to wars, persecutions, slavery, xenophobia, racism and chauvinism. The point is not to correct the mistakes and be really right; rather it is not to think you are right at all.' It is the claim to be right that is such an affront to modern tolerance. It is the claim to be right which so distresses writers like John Hick. But is he not guilty of precisely the same intolerance? He accepts all faiths, *except* the biblical revelation, and he clearly thinks he is 'right' in so doing.

But is he? What if there is a living God who made this world and all that is in it? What if he does love us with

an everlasting love despite all the rebuffs we give him? What if he did come to show us what he is like? What if he did stoop to burden himself with all our moral filth? What if he does offer the power of resurrection life to all of whatever faith and none, who will accept it? There is a massive truth question here, and it will not go away.

For beneath all the talk about openness and toleration there is a disturbing possibility: that people may base their lives on a lie, or that present patterns of oppression may continue and be justified upon the basis of beliefs that are false. To quote Alister McGrath again, 'Even the most tolerant pluralist has difficulties with that aspect of Hinduism which justifies the inequalities of Indian society by its insistence upon a fixed social order. Even the most tolerant of individuals finds difficulty in justifying the Hindu practice of forcibly burning alive a widow on her late husband's funeral pyre.' Were the British 'wrong' to put an end to this practice in the nineteenth century? On pluralist principles they were. Can you believe *that*?

It is in this area of truth that the pluralist position is so weak and unconvincing. In the end, the only reason for accepting the Christian gospel (or any other conviction for that matter) is not because it is culturally inherited, or politically correct or socially convenient: *but because it is true*.

6. *Pluralism is destructive of the Christian gospel.* This liberal pluralism, put forward with the best of motives by some well-intentioned Christian writers, ends up by destroying Christianity itself. It does so in two ways.'

First, it shows itself willing to abandon all the Christian distinctives which cannot be assimilated into other worldviews. In so doing, it abandons the core of the gospel. For in what other faith do you hear of the divine coming to seek you out, burdening himself with your wickedness in order to release you from it, breaking the death barrier, and offering to come and take up residence within you? Those are essential Christian distinctives. You have to abandon them all if you are going to move wholeheartedly into the pluralist camp. It is often done covertly, and with endless equivocations, but that abandonment of basic Christianity takes place. The fact is that Jesus is not in the least like any other religious leader who has ever lived. Christianity is Christ. So the pluralists have to cast doubt on the deity of Jesus, his achievement on the cross, and the fact of his resurrection, if they are even to put forward their case. That does not interpret or modify Christianity. It abolishes it.

Second, pluralists destroy Christianity by substituting religious experience for biblical witness as the criterion of belief and behaviour. They locate truth in altered consciousness rather than in a historical event. So we are saved not by God's grace but by our knowledge. Schopenhauer said as much in the nineteenth century. So did the Gnostics in the third. So did Plato in the fourth century before Christ. The God of grace, of transcendence, of intervention, is jettisoned.

There is an evident loss of transcendence in the theological fashions of the day, be it process, liberationist, feminist or neo-mystical theology. It is a dangerous tendency. They all offer us a religion where human experience and imagination replace divine revelation.

It has been pointed out that this situation has close parallels with Germany in the 1930s. The German Church had become very allergic to the idea of revelation. Scripture was seen not as God's thoughts about humanity, but our thoughts about God. Other human insights had equal validity. Scripture was replaced by the Volksgeist, the spirit of the age, leaving no standard by which to confront the increasingly totalitarian state. Some went as far as to remove Jewish expressions from the New Testament. Others saw God as androgynous. The occult flourished in Nazi Germany, as did nature

mysticism. The destructive and demonic side of religion
was conveniently overlooked. Any absolute claims to
truth were laughed to scorn. Even the Evangelical
Church of Germany wilted before the forceful paganism
of Hitler. It was only the Confessing Church, radical in
obedience, scriptural in norms, courageous in persecution, which withstood the avalanche and survived to
bring in a new day. And although the political scene is
very different in Western Europe today, the inner weakness and rottenness of what was once Christendom is
plain for all to see. The enfeebled pluralist Christianity
of our day will not need persecution to end it: its collapse
will come from within. It is self-destructive.

The battle is on. It lies between historic Christianity
with its belief in the reality of a supernatural God and
the uniqueness of his Son Jesus, and the new spirituality
which is embodied in many of the recent theological
fashions and religious movements, along with the New
Age. It is the battle between monotheism and pantheism,
between a catholic evangelicalism and a neo-Gnosticism.
One side defends both the particularity of divine revelation and the universality of its offer and its claims. The
other champions an homogenising global religious vision. We have to choose.

Christian Confidence in an Age of Pluralism

How can we Christians hold our heads high in a climate
like this? I close this chapter with three grounds for the
confidence which I have in a full-blooded New Testament
Christianity.

The first is *historical*. So much religious talk is like
soap in the bath. You cannot get hold of it. But with
authentic Christianity you can. It is totally dependent on
what happened 1,950 years ago. It is totally dependent on
the person and achievement of Jesus of Nazareth. Take

Jesus away from the centre of Christianity and the whole thing collapses like a pack of cards. Many, many people have tried to do just that, and they have failed. Jesus' bold claim to be the way to God, the truth about God and the very life of God has not been dislodged. The evidence about Jesus on which Christian belief rests has been more carefully sifted than any other evidence in all history. Yet the person, the teaching, the claims, the death and the resurrection of Jesus remain like a great offshore rock which all the fury of the waves down the centuries has been unable to smash. In that rock lies the nub of the whole Christian faith. It is impregnable.

My second ground for confidence is *rational*. There is a tremendous rationality about historical Christianity. It makes sense of man and nature, God being the author of both. It makes sense of both our moral and religious instincts, anchoring them in ethical monotheism. It makes sense of reason – a God-given faculty which is nevertheless subordinate to God. It makes sense of beauty, truth, goodness, creativity, communication, activity, leisure, play, love – anchoring them all as aspects of the God and Father of Jesus Christ, who exemplified them all perfectly during his life on earth. It makes sense of our awesome dilemma: how can a holy God tolerate unholy people like us? How can he have us back without compromising his holiness? It makes more sense of sin and suffering than any other faith. It has proved the spur for exploring God's world, for concerning ourselves with ecology as stewards of God, for education, peace, justice, medicine, care for the needy and helpless and the unborn. All these concerns spring from the very heart of the Christian God. It makes sense of the origin of the world, shrouded though that is in mystery. It makes sense of the laws of physics. It makes sense of other faiths – not ways of salvation, but often pointers to salvation: what Karl Barth called 'little lights' and 'other true words'. It makes sense of particularity and universality – God's grace available to all yet brought by one. It is coherent. It makes sense at a profound level, in a way that the New Age with its contradictions and pluralism, with its intellectual shallowness does not. It makes sense. That is what gives me confidence.

My third ground for confidence is *empirical*. Christianity works. All over the world, in all manner of cultures, you find the transformation that Jesus brings. To be sure, it is only partial in this life, but its lineaments are always the same. The direction moves from crime to caring, from lies to truth, from drunkenness to sobriety, from materialism to generosity, from self-centredness to service. The movement may be slow, for human nature is rugged, intractable stuff. But the direction is always the same. That is what gives me confidence. When I have the joy of leading someone to the feet of Jesus, I do not think or hope, I *know* that so long as they keep in touch with

Christ they will grow in his likeness – and he, remember, is the ideal for human life. They will move towards that goal. They will become more deeply and fully human, the being they were intended to become.

Other faiths produce saints from time to time, and that is wonderful. It generally happens after profound searching and meditation and self-discipline on the part of the disciple. But it is the supreme glory of Jesus that he takes all sorts, often from the very cesspools of society, and shows in them the fragrance of his new indwelling life. He, not the disciple, is the main agent at work. He is gradually restoring to that man or woman the divine image implanted originally by God but marred by the Fall. There will be many a failure, many a fall, but the changes become more and more evident down the years. Jesus is in the life-changing business. I know whom I have believed, and I am not ashamed of the gospel which always has been and still remains the agency of that transformation.

6

Apologetics in the Life of the Church

Apologetics is notable largely for its absence from the life of the modern Church. This is in striking contrast to a few decades ago, when towering figures such as C. S. Lewis, Cecil Day Lewis, Dorothy L. Sayers, J. R. R. Tolkien and T. S. Eliot made their presence felt within a Church which realised the importance of apologetics. Today, we are much worse off. Part of the explanation for this is the increasing pace of secularisation. But this is only part of the story.

Two prevailing attitudes have developed within the Church during the last twenty years, each with little time for apologetics. The liberal attitude is committed to dialogue – more specifically, to a type of dialogue which explores other people's views, but makes no attempt to get them to change their minds. A more conservative attitude is committed to preaching and other forms of direct evangelism, and tends to regard apologetics as a waste of time. This approach regards the human mind as fatally infected by the Fall. Preaching is the God-given way of allowing divine light to reach such people. Neither group, in consequence, has much time for apologetics. And over the course of a few decades, this has created serious problems.

It affects the clergy, who do not learn how to argue for

the faith, as well as proclaim it. As a result, the increasingly large secular population, who have never been reached by anything specifically Christian, see no good reason why they should change their minds about this matter. They remain unpersuaded.

It affects the laypeople in congregations, who grow less and less sure of what they believe. There is a growing chasm between the worlds of faith and reason. For this reason, Christian observance often only applies to Sunday mornings, and has little effect on our thinking and our lifestyle for the rest of the week.

It affects the theological seminaries. There are hardly any theological colleges or seminaries in which apologetics features as a proper, well-taught subject on the programme. Yet what could be more important than being able to give a good reason for our beliefs in a world which sees no *a priori* grounds to accept them? It is to me an astonishing mark of the backwardness of English theological education that we continue as if England were still a Christian country. We pay scant attention to evangelism and apologetics, two vital elements of the ever-growing missionary requirements of the Church.

So how can things be changed for the better? What is the agenda for churches who want to make sure that apologetics finds its place in their everyday life and witness?

Apologetics Integrated

It is essential that apologetics should be integrated into the teaching and ministry of the churches – something which the mainstream churches have generally failed to do. How can this best be done? I have been inquiring recently from some of the New Churches how they approach this whole area of teaching apologetics.

One major approach centres on an intensive course, of up to six weeks, usually associated with the attempt to plant a new church in the area. The first week is given to intensive training in the development of one's personal walk with God, informal worship, interdependence in a small group, and mutual ministry. Problems get sorted out, and hang-ups dealt with. There is a lot of interactive teaching on the nature of the gospel, how to initiate a conversation in a variety of situations, and how to face the most common objections to the good news of Jesus

Christ. There is some teaching in management skills, in telling one's spiritual story attractively and simply, with great stress being placed on the use of non-religious language.

People are given the opportunity to learn through role play. One effective method is to carry on from this beginning with an individual: 'You should be a Christian because . . .'. Another is to assume that someone comes up to you, saying something like this: 'I have noticed that there is something a bit unusual about you, and it seems to be linked up with this Christianity thing. Please tell me more.' Now you can scarcely have a clearer example than that of someone who is ready to respond to Christ!

But could you introduce such a person to the Lord? The young people on these practical, intensive training courses learn to do just that – something that many people who have been faithful church attenders for many years would probably not be able to do. The secret lies in *learning through doing* – in other words, apprenticeship. That is how the great artists and craftsmen of the Middle Ages were trained. In fact, even the clergy learned their skills in this way at that time. That is how the Hebrews trained people: a rabbi would take a group around with him, talk with them, and teach them all that he knew.

But we in the modern West have opted for a more Greek model of intellectual appreciation, rather than learning from discussing things with real people. As a result, we are ill-at-ease in an outreach situation. We have not been properly prepared for it. But these teams of young people give a few weeks of their summer to this apprenticeship in evangelism and apologetics. They live alongside their mentors in a church hall, where they sleep on the floor and cook their own food. They spend a good deal of time doing open-air ministry on the streets – amusing, outrageous, challenging. And that immediately gets them into a situation in which apologetics comes into play. They at once begin to put into practice what they have been learning, and come back to their tutors for more at the end of the day.

Here we find the constant interchange of learning and doing, individually and in a team, accompanied by living and working closely together in pursuit of a common goal. What a marvellous way in which to learn the trade! It is something to which working people can give two weeks in the summer. Students with longer vacations can offer more. This is certainly an approach that needs to be developed by the mainline churches.

Why? Because people see our church buildings, but would no more go into them than I would into a Masonic Hall. I would not know what to do. It is not my scene. I would feel uncomfortable. Thoughts very much like that go through the mind of non-churchgoers when you pester them to come to church with you. They think that church is for insiders, those who like that kind of thing. And if you are going to change their minds, they need to see Christians coming out from their ecclesiastical castles and doing their thing in the open air where they are not six feet above contradiction.

This coming out of the closet, so to speak, does two valuable things, even in a very short campaign. It shows people in the vicinity that Christians are alive and well – and fun! It shows that they are not afraid to stand up for Jesus Christ, and that they are keen to share what they have with all and sundry. That is quite an image breaker! And it is a lovely taste of active ministry, deep companionship, and reasoned faith for those who share in it. Many of them want more.

And more is provided. For example, Steve Clifford, a very experienced team director, heads up TIE ('Training in Evangelism') for the Pioneer group of New Churches. In addition to these short-term teams, he and his colleagues have a carefully-thought-out year-long training

programme, mostly in apologetics and evangelism,
through which they train young leaders. And I have to
say that very often these young leaders are more effective after a year of such training than a lot of ordinands
after three years in a theological college! They may not
know so much over such a range of subjects, but they
know the heart of the matter better, and how to apply it
to the needy people all round them, who are without God
and without hope in the world.

This year-long period of training, both intensive and
varied, concentrates on four areas in particular: lectures
and seminars, personal study, practical experience, and
personal development. All of these are undertaken within a fellowship of worship and ministry. Because most
Christian bodies do not train their leaders in this way, it
may be worth glancing a little more closely at what they
offer.

Currently, they have some sixty people in training,
with a full-time leadership of five, grouped in three
regions, each of which has a regional director. They
are placed in church planting situations, for the most
part, so that learning and doing can be readily combined,
and a new church possibly emerge from their efforts. A
core of experienced leaders works with them. Fifty days
in the year are devoted to intensive study. This is divided
into three residential periods, and other training days,
on some of which all sixty meet together. There are five
main sections of classroom work:

1. a foundational course in theology;
2. an overview of the whole Bible, with one gospel
   studied in depth;
3. careful teaching on all kinds of evangelism;
4. various aspects of the Christian life, including discipleship, spiritual gifts, sex, money, time management,
   team work, and prayer;
5. the world, with at least some attention to green issues,

cults, matters of race, colour and gender, youth culture, missions, and church history.

In addition to this classroom work, time is assigned to personal study, reading, and assessment. Each student keeps a personal journal, and talks over its contents with a personal tutor from time to time.

All trainees are seconded to a local church in the region, where they are exposed to a variety of work and learn as much through carefully monitored experience as through classroom work. To avoid the dangers of inbreeding, each is given a taste of ministry in another country, and gets to experience large-scale conferences such as Spring Harvest. All work for a period with ACET, one of the leading Christian ministries to AIDS victims. Finally, considerable care is taken over the personal development of students through regular meetings with their tutors, the deepening of discipleship, and the monitored acquisition of apologetic and pastoral skills.

I believe that the New Churches have much to teach the old established churches in the areas of apologetics and evangelism. It is integrated with life, with practical experience, and with real people (rather than stereotypes). It is both demanding and fulfilling, and does not seem to lead to the sense of disenchantment which is so common in most residential British theological colleges. At any rate, it is a good beginning at equipping suitable people in the churches with an all-round Christian development, which includes apologetics, but does not concentrate upon it at the cost of worship, evangelism, fellowship and personal holiness. The New Churches, as they are the first to admit, are far from perfect – but they have regained a principle which most churches have lost. That may be one reason for their advance, not only in numbers and effectiveness, but also in the quality of their Christian lives.

Apologetics and Preaching

As we have seen, apologetics is generally missing from present-day preaching. Neither liberal nor conservative preachers have much time for it. Yet apologetics is a vital tool for strengthening the Christian faith of congregations, and enabling them to reach out confidently to their friends and neighbours with a gospel that can withstand the more common objections which they encounter.

So why is there this weakness in contemporary preaching?

One reason, as we have seen, is the lack of conviction among clergy that this is an important area of ministry. But there are other reasons. One is the prevalence of family services and communion services in many churches. In the case of the former, the talk is generally directed towards the young, or to the parents through the young. It is therefore fairly basic in content. At

communion services, the emphasis tends to fall on devotion rather than edification. In addition, in Anglican churches there is often strong pressure to preach on the epistle or gospel of the day, thus making any regular teaching about the truths of the faith problematic.

Another reason is the decline of the sermon as a means of communication. Nobody listens to anyone else for fifteen minutes or so undiluted in any other sphere of life. As a result, people don't develop the power of concentration needed to cope with it. In addition, preaching is often not assigned a position of prominence by many clergy, who throw their energy into committees, social or pastoral work, chaplaincies, or even further degrees. While there are some obvious exceptions to this rule, especially in nonconformist churches, the trend is undeniable. This is not an age of great preachers.

Again, preachers rarely seem to wrestle with great themes. If they do, they generally fail to communicate in ways that are memorable. I recall Bishop Walsham Howe commending a pastor in the East End of London for giving his working-class congregation a brilliant summary of Bishop Butler's *Analogy of Religion* in a style so simple and so memorable that none of them would be likely to forget it – without, of course, ever referring to Bishop Butler or his celebrated book! That is an art which was possessed to perfection by Jesus Christ, the greatest intellect this world has ever seen, who nevertheless spoke in parables, the force of which nobody could evade.

If these are some of the causes of our weakness in effective apologetic preaching, how can the situation be remedied? In a number of ways.

1. The most obvious is in the Church itself. Preaching needs to have well-digested and well-argued biblical teaching at its core. We are not in business to provide placebos, but to build strong Christians. And it is Scrip-

ture, thoroughly understood and attractively presented,
which provides nourishment for the souls of the congregation in a manner that nothing else can ever hope to
match. Preachers must take pains to work hard on their
sermons. They will be assiduous in visiting both within
Church circles and outside them, to see what the concerns are to which the good news needs to be related.
The good preacher will be a bridge between profundity
and relevance. Alas, so many achieve neither.

It is important for preachers to be *au fait* with the same
events, books, newspapers, plays or television programmes as their congregations, and to wrestle with
them as ways of using them as channels through which
the truth of God can find its entrance into hearts and

minds. There will be times when the people need to go away with a very clear understanding of how God has acted to meet us in our suffering, how he can accept us when we are so unacceptable, how we can be confident that he exists, and why we are quietly sure of the reality of life after death. These are vital things. They affect everyone. The preacher may not have much influence outside his or her flock – but the congregation will. Every Monday sees them scattered all over the neighbourhood in their places of work. How marvellous it would be if they went confident of where they stood as Christians and why. That should not be beyond the power of most preachers, if they take real trouble to apply the gospel to the questions that real people really are asking. An excellent idea here is to have courses of sermons from time to time, well advertised and custom made to address the needs of the locality. That is a great place for apologetics!

2. There is another whole dimension to apologetic preaching which needs to be considered. (However, it would be wise to forget the word 'preaching' in this context, as it is a massive turn-off for many people. It conjures up memories of dreary addresses, cold churches, antiquated clothes, and chewing gum in the choir seats. As a result of these folk memories, preaching is one of the most unpopular of all activities for many people.) What I have in mind is the presenting of the Christian faith in an attractive way on neutral ground. It may be a debate in a town hall or university lecture theatre. It may be an impromptu gathering at a funeral wake, or in a home discussion group. It may be at an event organised by Christians who are in good contact with people on the fringe. A speaker may have been invited to speak on a highly relevant and preferably *piquant* aspect of the Christian faith. I recall subjects like 'Choose freedom!', 'Is life worth more than the funeral expenses?', 'Why

bother with Jesus?', 'Can values stand when faith has crumbled?', and so on, drawing large crowds of interested inquirers. A church that is doing that sort of outreach will not lack inquirers coming within its doors to find out more about what makes it tick. And if there is a healthy visitation programme led by laypeople, and a willingness to discuss the faith in pubs, wine bars or working men's clubs, the news will soon get round. And increasingly that church will develop an interested

fringe of occasional visitors who can, with love, prayer and diligence, be won into wholehearted discipleship.

3. This leads into a third area of preaching, one with a noble history reaching back to Jesus and his apostles, but which seems to have fallen into disrepute today. I refer, of course, to open-air preaching. You will tell me that this has had its day. But this is not the case. Perhaps the old-fashioned type of open-air meeting is a thing of the past, with dreary-looking men urging all and sundry to prepare to meet their God. But that is not the only way of proclaiming the good news in the open air. It can be done by means of questionnaires, or by stopping and chatting to people at market stalls. It can have a tremendous effect if a baptism or eucharist is carried out in the open air; the opportunities for discussion afterwards with interested passers-by are considerable.

But the most obvious sort of open-air ministry is for a group from the church to go to a well-populated place, and draw a crowd through music, drama, dance, clowning or the like. In between the various items someone can explain, in the most down-to-earth language, the wonder of God's love and our need to make a response. If you try this, you will understand why apologetics is so important. You will be assailed from all sides with objections, ridicule, anger and interest. You will learn the questions that are on people's hearts. You will learn to distinguish the real issues from the smokescreens. You will find the agenda for a truly relevant apologetics. And gradually, you will get better and better at dealing with the issues, and have more and more impact.

Apologetics and Teaching

One of the gifts of the ascended Christ, according to Ephesians 4:11, is leadership in the Church: leaders exist not to do all the work themselves, but to equip their

fellow-Christians for their own ministries. Unfortunately, this happens all too rarely. Many Christians
restrict their church activity to Sundays, apart from
choir meetings on Friday evenings, and perhaps a
ladies' meeting midweek. That is to miss the tide.

I have found that committed members of congregations
are eager to learn and willing to sacrifice time and effort
in order to be of more use to their Lord. In a previous
parish, I recall starting with a twelve-week training
course for leadership in general. We had thirty people
in it, being a mixture of volunteers and those I had
approached personally. As a result, the key people in
the congregation were present. We looked at the universal imperative to be ministers of Christ, at mutual
ministry in the body of Christ, at helping others to faith,
and at growing in prayer and expectancy. Each evening
saw a time of worship led by one of the congregation,
followed by supper. The group was divided into smaller
sections, each of which was allocated a group tutor. In
this way, a large number of issues were tackled over the
course of three months. Every group with their tutor
found a weekend of outreach in which to go and assist in
another church. This proved to be a very valuable basic
training in leadership. On top of it, we were able to offer
supplementary courses in subjects as disparate as coun-
selling, New Testament Greek, drama and preaching. It
had a profound effect in building up the congregation –
so much so that it was adopted by the diocese.

Apologetics is a very necessary element in such equipping. You could lay on an eight-week course on the basic
elements of the Apostles' Creed. You could look at
different objections to belief in God. You could examine
current attacks on Jesus Christ, and especially his
resurrection. You could wrestle with issues of relativism, humanism, pluralism and many of the other current '-isms' that are idolatrous seducers from the one
true God. You could run a course on the different

streams that have made up the river of modern scepticism – and how to face them. You could look at some of
the most common cults which trouble the locality. You
could look at a series of ethical issues, or the New Age
movement. To have, for example, three eight-week
courses during the year on topics such as these could
do untold good in training the congregation.

Of course, it can be done in other ways. How about
using the CPAS video *Christian Basics*? Or the David
Watson video tapes on Christian essentials, entitled
Jesus Then and Now – older, but still very useful. These
raise all the most central apologetic issues. In the latter
case, there is twenty minutes of input from David
Watson before the discussion breaks out.

How about taking a significant book – such as Lesslie
Newbigin's *The Gospel in a Pluralist Society* (SPCK),
John Young's *The Case Against Christ* (Hodder &
Stoughton), or Alister McGrath's *Bridge-Building*
(IVP) – reading a chapter a week, then meeting to tease
out its implications?

There are many ways of going about it, but I doubt if
we shall change the face of modern Western societies
until teaching is taken seriously in our churches, and
people learn to be able to give a credible account of the
faith that is within them.

Apologetics Down the Street

If apologetics is to be any good, it must be earthed – that
is, it must touch ordinary unchurched people where they
are. One of the most effective ways of doing this was
discovered by accident by Michael Wooderson. It all
began with a man at a funeral saying, 'I wouldn't mind
finding out more about the Christian faith.' That man
was totally unchurched. He was not into reading books.
He was not into going to church either. So what was
Michael Wooderson to do?

It was then that Michael hit upon an idea, which has now become one of the most effective ways of combining apologetics and evangelism at street level in Britain. He himself would be the first to tell you that he was very influenced in his thinking and approach both by the Jehovah's Witnesses (who were very active in his area), and by James Kennedy's *Evangelism Explosion* (Coverdale House). Both, though coming from very different assumptions, used three important methods. One was *systematic visiting*, aimed at uncovering interest and taking it further. A second was *setting up study groups*, preferably in the homes of interested inquirers. The third was to *send the new converts out visiting* at an early stage, before they realised that churchpeople generally did not do this kind of thing!

He developed these three method into a simple and effective approach, which is described in his book, *The Church Down Our Street* (Monarch Publications). Michael himself is gifted at making personal relationships. He discovers people in his area who would like to learn a little more about the Christian faith in the course of home visiting. However, he does not go himself; he sends in a small lay team, whom he has trained for the task. The idea is to aim for six visits, if all works out well, by a team of three persons from the church. (This number is significant: it allows inexperienced people to be trained on the job, and deepens fellowship within the church.) In the course of these visits, the church team give enough information to the people in the home to allow them to make an informed decision for or against Christ.

Of course, it is not all one-way teaching. It is full of discussion. The teaching itself is very basic, but the relationships are vital. Much depends on the quality of the first visit. If that goes well, those on the receiving end are generally intrigued, and keen to welcome the team back the following week. They are fascinated to see laypeople like themselves feeling so enthusiastic about the gospel that they are willing and able to take the time and make the effort to share it.

This is an evangelistic strategy and means of training in apologetics which is making a lot of headway in Britain, and has considerable potential for use elsewhere. Until recently, I taught evangelism in Canada. I found that this method is well received and widely practised amongst the most outward-looking Canadian congregations, and yields a very high proportion of positive responses to Christ, leading on to incorporation into the active life of a church. It would be invaluable in the context of the United States, to complement mass and lifestyle evangelism approaches. If you stop to consider the matter, you will notice that it combines several strands, each of which has a long history of use within the Church, but each of which, in isolation, has become tired and jaded – visiting, evangelism, home groups, lay training, apologetics, and nurture. These six strands, taken together and put into a highly flexible and people-centred package such as this, become a strong rope.

Another type of outreach also combines the making of relationships, the commending of the good news, the answering of difficulties, and the discovery of spiritual realities such as Scripture, prayer, fellowship and pastoral care. This is the 'discovery group' or 'nurture group', a short course of eight or so evenings, skilfully led in a relaxed manner for those who are feeling their way towards Christ, or have just become his followers. The ones in which I have been engaged for many years have been primarily directed towards those who have made some profession of faith, or want to do so. Given a group of eight such people, it would be normal to find that about half of them have taken the initial step of commitment to Christ in repentance and faith. The other half will not have done so.

On the first night, we all introduce ourselves and say

where we are on our journey of faith or unbelief. It is fascinating to hear the variety of positions along that road which are represented among those present. The one thing that you can be sure is that they will be in a different place in two months' time. Subjects such as Christian initiation, assurance, Bible reading, prayer, the Church, the sacraments, and Christian service are dealt with, at the rate of one an evening. There will be an appropriate passage of Scripture to be studied by the group. There will be a short talk, and wide-ranging discussion. There will be short, heartfelt prayers by the members as the evening draws to a close. There will be personal interviews at least twice during the course with one of the leaders. And suitable literature will be on sale, week after week.

In this caring environment of openness, clear presentation, and experience of answers to prayer, it is very easy for new converts to grow rapidly. This immediately challenges those who have not yet come to faith, because they can see the difference that faith makes to the others. They then need the quiet personal assistance and care of one of the leaders, who will explain that they cannot grow until they have been born, and that the new birth is God's gift to those who come in faith to Christ.

It will be clear that apologetics features prominently in this kind of evening. Those who come in from the cold, so to speak, will bring all manner of strange beliefs and preconceptions with them. The leaders will need all of their apologetic skills. But more than that – they need pastoral skills as well, in order to appreciate when they should speak, and when they should allow serious misconceptions to pass by unchallenged. I try to make a distinction between those misconceptions that are really troubling a person, and those which are simply part of his or her non-Christian baggage. It is the former that need tackling and addressing – the latter will fade away when they come to faith. Yet the former need not

necessarily be dealt with there and then. This could easily distract or divert the group from its agenda. They can be discussed privately later. I also occasionally take time within the group to discuss an objection or difficulty raised by one of them, if it seems to be the sort of thing that would be helpful to the group as a whole.

In these 'discovery' or 'nurture' groups, a number of people on the edge of the faith come to join it as the group life intensifies and the weeks pass by. An excellent example of how effective these groups can be is provided by the 'Alpha Groups' of Holy Trinity, Brompton, one of London's leading churches. They were designed as nurture groups for new Christians, with a sprinkling of 'not-yet-Christians' around as well. These rapidly became very popular, with attendance soaring into the hundreds. As a result, the groups soon changed in their nature. Instead of providing nurture for new Christians, they became transformed into the most effective apologetic and evangelistic agencies in the

church. People who had not yet come to faith were
attracted in large numbers. What was happening to
their friends? Where was this new joy coming from?
How had a totally new direction and discipline entered
their lives?

These were the sorts of questions raised by Alpha
Group members among their friends and acquain-
tances. So by the time one Alpha Group had ended,
there was a waiting list of new people seeking access.
That is how these groups grow. And naturally, they now
spend a lot of time in the first part of the course on basic
apologetics and explaining (and encouraging!) the way
to faith in Christ, before going on to build up the new
converts. Needless to say, Alpha Groups are catching on
in other parts of Britain. They have considerable potential for other urban areas in the Western world.

There are many other types of groups that churches
can arrange for agnostics. I have had the privilege of
leading a good many such groups. They are demanding,
and very rewarding. To offer such a group has many
advantages. It shows that you are not in the least afraid
to have your Christian faith subjected to honest inquiry
and sharp criticism. It attracts people who would not
normally be seen dead in church. It is normal for
members of the group to have been encouraged to attend
by family or friends who have been praying for them for
some time. It is great to have prayer support from an
interested party in the background. Another advantage
is that when those who have opposed Christianity are
converted, they usually become courageous and articulate advocates of the faith they once derided. So it is well
worth doing! Why not call such a group 'Agnostics
Anonymous', and inject that extra nuance of challenge? My friends Roger and Mushy Simpson have been
running these groups in Scotland as a regular part of
their programme for some years, and their church is
growing apace as a result.

These groups can be run in a number of ways. You might invite people round for supper on the first evening, and ask them what topics they would like to see included, making sure that you have one session dealing with the resurrection of Jesus, and another on the whole area of personal commitment. It is a great mistake to allow these evenings to touch the mind alone – they must also reach the will.

Another approach is to offer people a short course on basic Christian beliefs, giving reasons for your faith in God, in the divinity of Jesus Christ, and your conviction that the Spirit of God is still available to enter the lives of those who welcome him. You will need to have sessions on suffering, other religions, and the Church. You will also need to allow ample time for discussion of the subjects to be covered, and all sorts of things that are likely to emerge during the course.

Another way is to use appropriate video material, such as David Watson's *Jesus Then and Now*, the video tape of personal testimonies produced by the Anglican Diocese of Guildford in England, or the material provided by the *Gossiping the Gospel* resource, produced by the Uniting Church of Australia. Use the video as an introduction to the evening, and move on from there to the discussion that will inevitably arise. Some video packages provide helpful guidelines on how to respond to some of the issues which will arise, as well as indicating useful discussion starters for nervous leaders.

Yet another approach is to use inductive Bible study, such as Dick Lucas' course on Mark's gospel entitled *Read, Mark, Learn!*, or the material developed by the Navigators, as presented in Jim Petersen's *Evangelism for our Generation* (Navpress), which has an excellent appendix giving a step-by-step investigative Bible study of John's gospel.

In the end, it is not critical what course you use, or whether you make up your own. What *is* critical is the way in which you approach it. As stressed throughout this book, relationships are of vital importance to effective apologetics. You need to build good, warm, honest and caring relationships with all the people in the group. Without this, you will get nowhere. Given this, you can probably make endless mistakes, and be forgiven! I have found it important to make the aim of such a course abundantly plain. It is not yet another vague discussion about religion. Rather, it is an investigation into who Jesus is, and the challenge that he offers us. This enables you to keep the discussion coming back to Jesus and the resurrection, however wide-ranging the discussion may be.

Needless to say, the ambience of the meeting is of major importance. It is important that the atmosphere should be warm and hospitable, combining tough wrestling with truth with great consideration and love towards all the people who are present. Scripture has a power all of its own; those present may well be largely ignorant of it. It is thus important to get people's noses into the appropriate parts of the Bible, and come alongside them as a fellow seeker after truth, not as someone who professes to know it all.

Finally, all present need to be really honest in facing up to the evidence, even if it leads straight into the arms of the Jesus whom they have been so eagerly seeking to avoid. And I make it a practice to end the evening with prayer. This need not be a threat to anyone. I say, 'Here is a prayer which any agnostic can pray: but it is also a prayer which could open you up to the living God, if he exists. "O God, if you exist, please show yourself to each of us in this room who does not know you, and make us willing to entrust our lives to you if, and only if, we are persuaded by the evidence we shall examine each week".'

Three other important pieces of advice can be given, in bringing this section to a close. I have found the following important in running such groups.

First, I need to pray, and get others to pray. That is probably the most important thing of all.

Second, I need to get my 'clients' to do some homework. I give them an attractively-produced copy of a gospel to read through, and a book such as *You Must Be Joking* (Hodder & Stoughton) or *Who is this Jesus?* (Hodder & Stoughton), which I have written myself, or *Mere Christianity* by C. S. Lewis (HarperCollins), or *The Case Against Christ* by John Young (Hodder & Stoughton). That will get to them between meetings!

Third, I need to give careful thought and planning to each meeting, leaving people the maximum possible time to express their doubts, discovering which members of the group are the ones to concentrate on and which to let fly by, and making sure that when I do not know an answer I admit it at once, and offer to come back with some research on the subject next week.

One thing I can guarantee. If you run groups like this, your apologetics will be constantly sharpened and upgraded in the best of all training schools – that of front-line experience!

7

Apologetics Among Those Who Rarely Read

Culturally, we are in a remarkable situation. Despite all the educational advances in the Western world, a growing proportion of the population rarely reads. To give an example: statistics indicate that 9% of the British population are still functionally illiterate at the age of eighteen. That amounts to nearly five million people! And even more than this do not have *any* books in their possession, and do not read a book from one year's end to another. Their reading is confined to work manuals, bills, cook books, and the tabloid press.

I have been reading the tabloid press recently, and am profoundly impressed by the skills which it displays. The size is accessible, the cost is right, the headlines are bold, and the tone is warm. And though the stories are often scurrilous, they are almost all personal stories, keyed in to the interests of the readers. (There are strong parallels with Scripture here! Perhaps as much as 70% of the biblical material is cast in the form of arresting and thought-provoking personal stories.) There is little abstract thought, but usually a lot of sharp intelligence, and frequently bold editorial comment. Those who try to reach this section of the British population with the good news have an enormous amount to learn from the *Mirror* and the *Sun*. When I was principal of a British

theological college, I used to get the editor of the *Mirror*
to the college every now and then to provoke the
students and sharpen them up. It was always an outstanding occasion. He would then take one or two of the
most promising communicators, and put them alongside
the *Mirror* trainees in journalism for a week or so. It was
a real shock to them to see how the lead article of around
250 words went through six or eight revisions before it
hit the press. If we took that amount of trouble with our
preparation, we might find our communication more
effective.

I am not aware that anyone has really mastered the art
of effective and life-changing communication of the
gospel with those who rarely read. But it is absolutely
vital that we try. After all, the first Christians were for
the most part illiterate. In many parts of the world today
in which the gospel is spreading fast, people cannot read.
We ought to be able at least to examine some principles
which are relevant to this, the biggest difficulty which
confronts the progress of the gospel in the developed
countries of the West.

It is important at this point to recognise some of the
general differences in ways of learning between those for
whom the written word is a comfortable medium, and
those for whom it is not.

People with developed literacy tend to think in
straight lines of connected reasoning. They keep dia-
ries, and plan things in advance. They are at home with
theoretical and abstract ideas. They have a planned and
structured training, and study on their own without
needing constant supervision. Their outlook and emphasis is individualistic. Their friends tend to be of similar
class and occupation – often widely separated, in different parts of the country. They are men and women with
degrees, career prospects, and high mobility.

In contrast, people who can read but rarely do, often
think in a non-linear manner, with the mind jumping

from one thing to another. They are spontaneous and impulsive. They think concretely and in pictures. They learn empirically, and in groups rather than by solitary study. Their emphasis is collective rather than individualistic, in order to ensure improvement in wages and conditions. Their friendships tend to be local – in the same street, club and pub. Their skills are manual, rather than academic. They often remain in more-or-less the same part of the country all their lives, in contrast to the much higher mobility of those with degrees.

These are some of the general differences between these two groups of people. They are radical. And so is the understanding of the gospel associated with each group. The minister – who is almost invariably a literate person – may well be concerned with doctrinal orthodoxy, church tradition, and the content of the gospel. The less literate person is much more concerned with what's in it for him and his mates. He wants to see the gospel in action, and expressed in ways that connect up with his experience of life. Indeed, even the implications of the gospel are seen very differently. The literate tend to express these in terms of individual conversion and individual growth in grace thereafter. Is it any wonder that those who depend upon collective action and group solidarity assume that the gospel is not for them?

I have a great deal to learn in this area. In Britain, people like Eric Delve and Dan Cozens have pioneered in the area of evangelism and apologetics among the less literate. In what follows, I also owe a lot to people like John Oliver, Roy Dorey, Neville Black and others in the Evangelical Urban Training Project. The general principles which emerge from their experience can be summarised as follows.

Apologetics through Relationships

Those who communicate by letter and phone need to

learn to communicate by being together with those whom they hope to help – and in settings where the latter feel at home and can call the shots. That is perhaps one of the greatest weaknesses of our middle-class churches. They become ghettoes, in which folk find their friendships and social life, and do not have to break out to those who live and think differently. Yet however different your background, you may help less literate people to come to Christ if you love them and spend time with them. The pub may not be my natural watering hole – but it had better become so if I want to influence working people for Christ.

Nobody has grasped that principle more firmly than Dan Cozens, with his imaginative 'March of a Thousand Men'. A large contingent of Christians spend weeks walking along some of the most scenic routes in England, along the Pennines or down in Cornwall. They spend a lot of time in the pubs, talking with the regulars there. This leads to interest, lively discussion, and many commitments to Christ. It enshrines, in its own distinctive way, the basic principle of the incarnation. God loves the world so much that he did not send a telecast but his Son to be among us! We must make sure that we *meet* people where they are. They cannot know what you are really like until they meet you. And so relationship is the single most crucial principle for reaching those who rarely read. They will certainly not read our books!

Friendship is an important aspect of this business of forming relationships. Everyone values friends. If we can both display friendship and point to the 'friend who sticks closer than a brother', we shall cut ice. But it will take time. That is why it is so essential for those seeking to be effective in this sort of culture to stay put, get known, form relationships and prove dependable over many years if the fruit is to come. I was given a marvellous story by John Oliver, a remarkable Scripture Union worker living in West Ham, London. There was a group of boxers in the area, drinking whisky. A vicar passed by. They shouted at him, 'Have a swig!' He did. And he thus began a friendship with them, even though they were worlds apart in their backgrounds. Three years later, one of them came to Christ. Five years later, another. Ten years later, a third. All because he stopped and had a drink from their bottle of communal whisky. One is now a very sharp boxing promoter at the ripe old age of twenty-eight. Someone challenged him recently, asking him: 'Jesus said, "Turn the other cheek." How do you reconcile that with boxing?' The answer came like a flash: 'First, I'm not Jesus. Second, I've only been a Christian six months. Don't trust your luck!'

Friendship also serves two additional purposes. It *offers encouragement*, especially important in a world in which hope and joy are noticeably absent. Befriending people can open doors to the future. It can lead to their regaining confidence and self-respect. And, perhaps most important of all, it models the way in which Christ

befriended, accepted and loved those who had been written off by the world. And it *offers the gospel through friendship*. For some of these people, their Christian friends will be the only way they have of gaining access to the gospel. They don't read; but they can watch and listen. Sometimes this friendship will remind them of their Christian heritage, somewhere in the distant past. It may encourage them to pick things up, and start again. Or the friendship may be the first contact they have with Christianity embodied in a real life. By telling their stories, Christians can make a deep impact on this group of people. Which brings us to our next point for discussion . . .

Apologetics through Stories

What sells local newspapers? Stories. What will you hear in any bar? Stories. And what literary form is predomi-

nant in the Bible? Once again, it is the story. The Bible is
by far the best and most exciting story book in the world.
It is also the most varied. And yet we so often manage to
turn its pages into a quarry for doctrine! The Hebrew
language, in which so much of the Bible is written, is a
language of action, with lots of verbs. We have turned its
contents into a language of theory, with lots of abstract
nouns! We have departed from the Hebrew roots of our
Christian heritage, and adopted Greek approaches instead. And we need to repent of this! We also need to
become expert once again in the art of story telling.
Currently we use the story as an illustration of some
abstract or doctrinal point we are making. And then we
try to apply it – and at once make the story boring, and
lose the attention of our audience. We need to give a
much higher priority to stories as such in our communication. Think of Dr Paul White, telling his Jungle
Doctor stories to an excitedly attentive crowd in the
mystery of an African night. Think of Eric Delve, one of
the best Christian communicators in Britain today. How
does he communicate so effectively? With stories. Think
of Jesus himself, the most spell-binding of all story
tellers, on the hillsides and shorelines of Palestine. We
need to learn from them!

Story telling is not all speech on our part. We need to
develop a genuine interest and enjoyment in listening to
other people's stories. We need to help members of our
churches to articulate their stories if they are to become
effective agents of evangelism in our society. And we
need to pay attention to the local and cultural factors
that influence the lives – and stories – of ordinary people.
Above all, we need to immerse ourselves in the stories of
the Bible, which are so often unknown today. For the
story is so often sufficient in itself. It does not always
need a postscript from us. Jesus constantly used stories
in this way – *and he refused to explain them*! He left
people to wrestle with the enigmas which they embodied,

confident that this would bring them to a more considered and wholehearted response in due course. We need
to feel our way into the biblical stories, make them our
own, and communicate them with verve and relevance
when the moment is right. Telling *our* story and *his* story
are two things we can all do – if we work at it.

Apologetics through the Visual

Even highly literate people are reckoned only to absorb
about 20% of what they hear in a connected discourse.
But if it is illustrated by some visual material, that
proportion may well be tripled. We need to make use of
the visual. This, alongside the relationship factor, may
help to explain the effectiveness of Anglo-Catholic
clergy in the East End of London. People may not
understand – or care much about – their theology. But
their presentation of the faith is highly visual – and it
communicates. We need never be afraid of the appeal of
mystery in this deeply pragmatic age. It is in such short
supply that it often has an irresistible impact on people
whose souls are made for it, but are starved of it.

The greatest medium of communication today is entirely visual – television. So central has it become to the
vast bulk of humanity that for many societies in the
world, literacy may soon become an irrelevance. You can
move from a jungle culture to a television culture without ever having to learn to read. The book is not a
necessity. If we want to communicate the faith effectively to a non-book culture, we need to make effective
use of television whenever we get the opportunity.

But the mass media alone will never suffice to spread
the faith. Spreading the faith is something incarnational,
something which needs a personal touch. Most of us
communicate effectively to relatively few people at once.
We shall be wise to think how we can give a visual
presentation to them – not just to the children, but to the

adults as well. We need to investigate the whole world of comics for adults, which is a major industry in the United States and elsewhere. Think of *The Gospel According to Peanuts* and its impact if you need to be convinced of the importance of encouraging and developing top-grade graphic artists within the Christian community. We need more Delia Smiths and Galloping Gourmets with their cookbooks and blazing Christian faith. We need people to set out the Christian story diagrammatically, with short, clear script – like a maintenance manual on a car. Just think of the millions of copies that the evangelistic booklet *Journey into Life* has sold, largely because it is short, clear, and above all *visual*. Or think of the way in which Lion Publishing has carved out an entirely new secular market with its clear themes and visual impact. There is room for a great deal of development in this area.

Music is, on any showing, one of the most potent means of communication in a culture. The message we bring can be further enhanced if it is commended through music as well as words, and preferably music which has a visual aspect (such as a soloist or orchestra). A singer such as Cliff Richard, moving through his secular into his Christian repertoire, and pausing from time to time to speak of his encounter with Christ, is wonderfully effective in arguing the cause.

Drama is another obvious way of making a direct point with one of those powerful three-minute sketches which were pioneered on the streets by the acting group Riding Lights in the 1960s, and are widely used throughout the world today. It is very effective to weave a couple of sketches into a speaking presentation, and increasingly evangelists are coming to value it as a most helpful tool. But it can also serve an apologetic purpose, if the sketch deals with some difficulty or tackles some problem head on. Whether in the streets and parks, in churches or in evangelistic outreach, drama is a marvellous way to

complement the spoken word, and it always draws a crowd.

Another resource, the potential of which we have been slow to appreciate, is mime. It is more effective because it is not dependent upon words. It is therefore truly cosmopolitan, and can communicate in any culture. We need to encourage such artists and work with them. If not, we shall never reach the non-literary folk of whom there are so many in our modern Western society.

Apologetics through Life-Experience

All those working among the non-reading population are agreed that the best way of communicating is through life-experiences. Roy Dorey tells of some of the ways he has found helpful in this respect. He might get a group to talk about the dilemma of making choices – a universal experience. From that, it is actually not difficult to get to the incarnation – God, too, has to make choices. You can get abstract ideas to come alive in a group of people who rarely read.

Roy argues that everyone has experiences connected with death, suffering, hope, justice, love and forgiveness. First, he asks people what they believe about one of these issues. This is followed up with a discussion about how they came to hold these beliefs. At this point, Roy shows people how Jesus and one of the stories he told relates to this issue. Finally they go on to explore the difference it makes to the way they live.

Apologetics through the Group

Our literate post-Enlightenment individualism is not going to get through to the collectivism of non-literate people. Even if it were successful, it would simply cut them off from their mates. You need to deal with the group. To be sure, find and go for the leader – but deal with the group. This will demand qualities which are not always found in evangelists and apologists. It will mean the readiness to affirm and tolerate diversity of opinion within the group. It will mean the readiness to affirm and encourage people, so that they feel confident enough to formulate their questions about Christianity. It also means having a genuine respect for them, and where they are coming from. It will mean having a sense of what is going on in people and between people in a group. It will mean being able to work with a group in such a way that it comes to its own conclusions and decides on its own actions. 'Everyone,' says Roy Dorey, 'is a treasure chest of information and experience. Our task is to give people the keys to undo their treasures.' And if the Christian worker has to change in order to reach such people, just think how much most churches are going to need to change before they can serve the local community in deprived areas, and ones in which literacy is not a highly valued skill. It is going to require a revolution. It is going to require an incarnation . . .

Apologetics through Personal Discovery

In literate circles, we are accustomed to making decisions based upon what we have read, reflected on, or been told by a reputable authority. In less literate circles, the discovery is the key – finding out by experience how a thing works. Thereafter, it is embedded in the memory, repeated in a variety of circumstances, and built into life. We want their Christian faith to be like that. It would be a lot richer than much of our experience. But we have to give them the tools to make the discovery themselves, not just as individuals, but as a group.

I wish I knew better how to bring that about! But I can think of occasions on missions when I have seen it happen. I recall one group of hooligans (all of whom had crossed swords with the police, and most of whom had spent time in jail), who came to make fun of us and rough us up as we proclaimed the gospel in the streets. They tried to destroy our visual aids, and break up our meetings. They were met with firmness and love. At the end of the two weeks, we had an amazing meeting at which the leader and many of his mates entrusted their lives to Christ. The mayor of that city had also been converted. So I got him to meet them, and listen to their problems, which he had legislated against but not understood. Out of that mission a Christian youth worker emerged. And the sequel was the city making over a property in the city centre for this group of youths to have a club, which was staffed by this Christian youth worker, who left his old job to join this new venture. It showed me the power of the gospel, and the importance of relationships and loving persistence. But it also brought home the need for a group to cohere and to make their own discovery of Christ in their own way at their own time.

I am still wearing my 'L' plates in this matter of trying to communicate the gospel effectively and argue its truth with those who do not use the medium with which I am most at home – the written word. I have a long way to go. But I know that it is one of the most important challenges facing apologetics and evangelism in our generation. I am determined to pursue it.

8

Moving On

As the second millennium of Christian existence comes to a close, our eyes turn towards the next thousand years of history. What lies ahead? Whatever the answer may be, apologetics is going to be of vital importance in the next ten or so years – a period which many churches worldwide have designated 'A Decade of Evangelism'. Here is a vision to inspire and challenge us.

Apologetics serves two purposes, as we have seen.

First, it allows people to recognise and appreciate the attractiveness of the Christian faith. For some, it is like blowing the dust away from an ancient mosaic, so that its beauty and glory can be seen. For others, it is like being given a pair of spectacles, which suddenly bring sharply into focus things which had been blurred. We have seen how care and consideration need to be given to individuals, so that the full wonder of the Christian faith may be focused on that person's special needs and hopes.

Second, it helps to remove barriers to faith. All kinds of obstacles come between people and faith – reasons of the heart, of the mind, and of culture. We can be far more effective in our witness to Christ in the world at large, if we take time to understand these general factors. However, we can be even more effective in our witness to our friends and loved ones, if we take the trouble to work out how these general principles relate to them as particular individuals. Everyone is different. Earlier, we used the image of a 'road to faith'. That road is littered with different obstacles for different people; we need to be sensitive to where people are. This book will help you identify some likely problem areas. It will allow you to work out how to respond to them. But the rest is up to you. You know your friends. How can you help them?

If you are able to help your friends and colleagues agree that Christianity is a profoundly attractive and viable option in the modern world, you will have achieved an enormous amount. And yet . . . something is missing. Agreement needs to lead on to personal commitment. How?

The Leap of Faith: From Agreement to Personal Commitment

Apologetics assures the world (and reassures Christians!) that Christianity is deeply attractive, and that it

possesses coherence and credibility. Having done that, it can do no more. Yet more needs to be done. To appreciate this point, let us look at the example of the person who faced up to the need for a next step: a step of faith.

Sheldon Vanauken is an American writer, who studied English Literature at Yale and Oxford Universities. Vanauken came to faith at Oxford in the spring of 1951, with some friendly guidance from C. S. Lewis. Yet coming to faith was a difficult decision. Vanauken's dilemma was this: Christianity made a lot of sense. But how was he to enter into it? How could he move from knowing that Christianity was right to being a Christian? As the Danish philosopher Søren Kierkegaard had pointed out, it was perfectly possible to know what Christianity was all about, without actually being a Christian. So how could this gap be bridged? How could someone move on from *knowing about* Christianity to *becoming* a Christian?

In his autobiography *A Severe Mercy* (Hodder & Stoughton), Vanauken describes with stunning clarity the kind of thoughts which go through many people's minds about the 'leap of faith':

How was I to cross it? If I were to stake my whole life on the risen Christ, I wanted proof. I wanted certainty. I wanted to see him eat a bit of fish. I wanted letters of fire across the sky. I got none of these. And I continued to hang about on the edge of the gap ... It was a question of whether I was to accept him – *or reject*. My God! There was a gap *behind* me as well! Perhaps the leap to acceptance was a horrifying gamble – but what of the leap to rejection? There might be no certainty that Christ was God – but, by God, there was no certainty that he was not. This was not to be borne. I could not reject Jesus. There was only one thing to do once I had seen the gap behind me. I turned away from it, and flung myself over the gap towards Jesus.

Vanauken here provides a brilliant statement of the dilemma that Christian apologetics will provoke, while at the same time solving it in a highly personal and memorable manner. The decision to believe breaks the paralysis of indecision which otherwise hovers around the gap of faith. Vanauken puts it like this:

> I *choose* to believe in the Father, Son and Holy Ghost – in Christ, my Lord and my God. Christianity has the ring, the *feel*, of unique truth. Of *essential* truth . . . [But] a choice was necessary; and there is no certainty. One can only choose a side. So I – I now choose my side: I choose beauty; I choose what I love. But choosing to believe is believing. It's all I can do: choose. I confess my doubts and ask my Lord Christ to enter my life. I do not *know* God is, I do but say: Be it unto me according to Thy will. I do not affirm that I am without doubt, I do but ask for help, having chosen, to overcome it. I do but say: Lord, I believe – help Thou my unbelief.

Vanauken appears to have stumbled upon one of the most powerful insights of the Christian faith. Coming to faith is about *our decision to believe* – at least, what seems to us, from our human standpoint, to be our decision.

So we can say to our friends: Choose to believe! Make that choice! Decide for Christ! And with that decision, the gap of faith is bridged. It is like someone reaching out and taking the bread that he senses is there. Or like Israel crossing the Jordan, and finally entering into that long-promised and long-hoped-for land.

From Apologetics to Evangelism

Apologetics makes the case for faith; evangelism makes the decision for faith. This analysis allows us to under-

stand some important points. First, the apologist need
not be an evangelist. As we have said, there is a natural
connection between them. However, the ordinary Christian believer may feel slightly apprehensive about putting his or her friends in a difficult position by asking
them if they would like to become Christians. Yet those
same ordinary Christians are doing a vital job – allowing
their friends to see the Christian faith in a new light.
One day, they may well decide to take that step of faith.
It may well be that someone else will help them take that
step of faith. One sows; another reaps (see 1 Corinthians
3:6). But this does not matter! What *does* matter is that
sowing and reaping go on!

Second, it shows how important apologetics is in the
ordinary life of the Church. Not only does it enable
people outside the churches to view Christianity more
positively, it also creates a climate of confidence within
the Church, by reassuring believers of the coherence,
credibility and relevance of their faith. And that needs to
be done! A lot of Christians are hesitant about their
faith, precisely because they lack confidence in it. Confidence and complacency are not to be confused! To have
confidence in the gospel is to have confidence in God, not
confidence in ourselves. One of the great insights of the
gospel is that God is able to take ordinary people, and do
the most extraordinary things through them – if we will
let him.

Third, it allows us to see the importance of a regular
evangelistic ministry in the local church. Many people
still think of evangelism as something that happens at
great rallies, organised by huge committees, and making
use of the talent of superstar performers. But evangelism
is something that can and ought to go on in every small
town Christian fellowship. Many Christians are apprehensive about this, feeling uncertain about how their
friends would respond to an evangelistic sermon or talk.
But one of the reasons why people feel apprehensive is

that, at the moment, this is something that is *unusual*. Apprehension here reflects the simple fact that evangelism has yet to find its way into the normal pastoral life and preaching of the local church. Churches will start to grow when people feel confident enough to begin to talk to their friends about their faith, to bring them to church to hear regular, competent presentations of the Christian gospel, and to respond to a sensitive and caring call for a personal decision to faith. Once this pattern becomes established in the life of a church, the potential for growth is enormous. It has yet to happen; but, given time and commitment, it will happen.

From Evangelism to Spirituality

Apologetics creates a favourable climate for faith. Evangelism brings people to faith. And finally, spirituality keeps people in faith. One of the most important developments in the life of the Church in the last twenty years has been the blossoming of interest in spirituality – that is, in ways of deepening one's faith through reading of Scripture, prayer, meditation, and all other proper means for Christians. In the past, the churches in the West tended to assume that the majority of the people were Christians. They didn't need to be evangelised; after all, they were all Christians anyway, weren't they? And they didn't need anyone to help them keep going in that faith, let alone to grow in faith. After all, whoever heard of someone stopping being a Christian? Sadly, complacency set in.

But not any more. The modern churches have finally realised that they need to identify and deploy every resource at their disposal, if they are to keep going and keep growing in the harsh, godless world of today. Apologetics, evangelism and spirituality are like the three legs of a stool, which bring stability to the life of the churches. Christian nurture groups have sprung up,

with the object of giving young Christians all the assistance and support that they need. A new emphasis has been placed on 'discipling' – the process by which 'converts' become 'disciples'. As the parables of Christ remind us, faith is like a plant – a plant which needs tending in its early stages, if it is to grow. Yet grow it will, leading to a new generation of mature Christians, who will be the future treasure and hope of the Christian Church.

For this reason, it is important that local churches give care and consideration to ways of deepening the faith of young Christians. And experience suggests that it is not simply those who are young in the faith who need help! Very often, older Christians find new depth coming to their Christian lives, as a result of attending courses intended for those who have recently come to faith. 'We never had these in our day,' one lady said to me appreciatively, as she revelled in discovering aspects of the Christian faith that were new to her. She was making up for lost time!

But our main concern must be those who come to faith for the first time. The powerful thrust of the Decade of Evangelism throughout the world runs the risk of being dissipated unless those who come to faith are kept in faith by every proper means of spiritual nourishment, encouragement and guidance. Some come to faith because of the power of an evangelistic sermon, delivered by a preacher skilled in the art of delivery and a master of the art of oratory. Yet the content of that sermon may live on only in the presence and personality of the preacher. The sense of immediacy, of personal dynamism and excitement, is lost once the preacher moves on. A new believer is left behind, to discover the full implications of that important decision to begin the Christian life and adjust accordingly. It is here that Christian spirituality has a vital role to play.

One of the most remarkable periods of renewal in the American Church took place in eighteenth-century Massachusetts. It initially centred on Jonathan Edwards, whose preaching was instrumental to the revival. At the height of the Great Awakening, a young woman convert wrote a letter to Edwards. She had come to faith; now she needed guidance, as she put it, as to 'the best manner of *maintaining* a religious life'. In that letter may be seen an anticipation of the modern realisation of the need for sustained follow-up in relation to evangelism. One of the most significant aspects of the Springboard initiative within the Church of England, headed by Michael Green and Michael Marshall, has been the realisation of the vital role of spirituality in a considered and realistic approach to evangelism. Spirituality is a means of keeping converts, and enabling them to grow in faith. The emphasis upon evangelistic techniques typical of the early 1980s is now being supplemented with a recognition of the need for the long-term spiritual care of those who come to faith.

At the practical level, this has many implications.

It means fostering the habit of *reading the Bible*. One of the most helpful ways of doing this for new believers is for an older Christian to spend time with them, and talk about a passage chosen for study. Parish, college and workplace Bible studies can be ideal places to help young Christians develop the habit of reading the Bible, and being nourished by what they find. All kinds of aids – such as commentaries and study notes provided by the Bible Reading Fellowship and Scripture Union – may be of use in this respect.

It means encouraging new believers to *go to church*. The Christian life is not meant to be lived in splendid isolation. The Church is a body, whose members are there to encourage one another, and to build one another up. The sermon provides a potentially vital resource for spiritual growth for new believers. The sacrament of baptism can be a powerful public declaration of one's new-found faith to friends and neighbours, as well as a great encouragement to other church members. The sacrament of holy communion can be a deeply moving reminder of the love of Christ for sinners, and an affirmation of his continuing presence in the Church. The fellowship provided by small groups within a church can provide a close and caring environment in which new believers can grow. Often, churches arrange such groups with the needs of such people in mind – such as Alpha Groups, as we have seen.

Finally, we need to *mentor* new believers – setting an example to them. Today's new believers are tomorrow's evangelists and church leaders. People learn by doing. Rembrandt and other great painters taught by personal example, allowing their apprentices to paint in areas needing large blocks of colour. The gospels show Jesus himself encouraging his disciples to learn by doing. The sequence of events in Luke 8–10 is especially interesting. In Luke 8, the disciples learn by watching Jesus preach, teach and heal. In Luke 9, he sends twelve of them out to begin to share in his ministry. They are given some personal responsibility. And in Luke 10, Jesus sends out seventy-two such disciples! That same pattern can be repeated today, as we try to encourage and teach by example. There is a vitally important role for both old and new believers in this task of looking ahead to the future.

And in the Long Term . . .

This book has tried to set out a vision of the importance of apologetics for ordinary Christians and ordinary local Christian churches. As we have emphasised, there is an enormous amount that can be done. The future wellbeing of the Christian churches depends upon Christians realising that they can do far more than they realise, without risking losing vital friendships or relationships. A recent English survey examined the way in which men came to faith. One of the most important routes was the personal witness of the women that they loved. Sharing their faith was, for them, an act of love – and, as the results show, in many cases this act of sharing was deeply appreciated.

We stand poised on the brink of the third millennium of Christian faith. An unknown future lies ahead. However, we do know that the same God who called his Church into being will remain with us, as we seek to serve him in the next millennium. We also know that the Christian future depends upon our willingness to tell others about the attraction and power of the gospel. We owe it to our future to begin this in earnest right now!

Resources for Apologetics

The present work has aimed to be free-standing. However, some readers may value guidance on additional resources. Three groups of resources will be noted briefly in this section.

Given the increasing importance of image-based apologetics, and the general shift away from a literature culture in the West, *video* material of direct apologetic and evangelistic relevance is noted.

Second, a select list of *books* of proven apologetic value is provided. All are currently in print, and readily available.

Third, a list of *institutions* which from time to time offer conferences, summer schools, extension studies or distance-learning programmes in Christian thought – including apologetics – is provided.

This resource list does not aim to be exhaustive. It simply aims to illustrate what is available. Your local Christian bookshop will be able to provide further guidance and information.

Videos

The following have proved to be especially useful for apologetics and evangelism training sessions, and for leading apologetic or evangelistic discussion groups.

Christian Basics: *A Journey to Faith* (1991). Church Pastoral Aid Society, Athena Drive, Tachbrook Park, Warwick, CV34 6NG, United Kingdom.

Gossiping the Gospel (1990). Uniting Church Board of Mission, PO Box E178, St James, NSW 2000, Australia.

It's No Good Shouting! (1992). The Gospel and Our Culture, Selly Oak Colleges, Bristol Road, Birmingham B29 6LQ, United Kingdom.

Jesus Then and Now (1982). Trinity Trust, PO Box 5, Hay-on-Wye, Hereford, HR3 5BP, United Kingdom.

Journey into Life: The Video (1988). Sunrise Video, PO Box 814, Worthing, West Sussex, BN11 1TSW, United Kingdom.

Person to Person (1986). Bible Society, PO Box 240, Swindon SN5 7HA, United Kingdom.

Saints in Evangelism: The Training Video (1991). Anglican Renewal Ministries, 45 Friar Gate, Derby, DE1 1DA, United Kingdom.

Books

A full list of books dealing with apologetics may be found in: McGrath, Alister, *Bridge-Building: Effective Christian Apologetics* (Leicester: Inter-Varsity Press, 1992).

For a full discussion of the theoretical and practical aspects of evangelism at the local level, see Green, Michael, *Evangelism through the Local Church* (London: Hodder & Stoughton, 1989).

For a careful study of how people come to faith, which reveals the important role played by personal relationships, see: Finney, John, *Finding Faith Today: How Does it Happen?* (Swindon: Bible Society, 1992).

A study guide to this survey, especially useful for church study groups, is also available: Young, John, *Journey into Faith* (Swindon: Bible Society, 1992). Both these are essential reading for churches considering serious involvement in the Decade of Evangelism initiative.

Those wanting to understand the shifting cultural background against which apologetics takes place should consult:

Montefiore, Hugh (ed.), *The Gospel and Contemporary Culture* (London: Mowbrays, 1992).

Newbigin, Lesslie, *The Gospel in a Pluralist Society* (London: SPCK, 1989).

The following provide easy-to-read approaches to issues that are of central importance to popular apologetics – such as the resurrection, the divinity of Christ, and so on. They are essential reading for those involved in any kind of apologetic ministry, especially among students.

Gaukroger, Stephen, *It Makes Sense* (London: Scripture Union, 1991).

Green, Michael, *You Must Be Joking!* (London: Hodder & Stoughton, 1981).

Green, Michael, *The Dawn of the New Age* (London: DLT, 1993).

McGrath, Alister, *Explaining Your Faith Without Losing Your Friends* (Leicester: Inter-Varsity Press, 1989).

Weston, Paul, *Why We Can't Believe* (Leicester: Inter-Varsity Press, 1991).

Young, John, *The Case Against Christ* (London: Hodder & Stoughton, 1986).

Resource Institutions

The main body devoted to fostering apologetics during the Decade of Evangelism is the Springboard initiative of the Archbishops of Canterbury and York. (The present book arose out of its first conference.) Its conferences on apologetics and evangelism are open to all interested, irrespective of denomination. Details may be obtained from:

Springboard
9 The Precincts
Canterbury
Kent
CT1 2EE
UK

Many other institutions offer suitable resources from time to time; the following are typical.

US and Canada

Regent College	Fuller Seminary
5800 University Boulevard	Pasadena
Vancouver	CA 91182
BC V6T 2E4	USA
Canada	

International Christian magazines, such as *Christianity Today*, provide details of major upcoming conferences and conventions well in advance.

Australia

Moore College	Ridley College
1 King Street	160 The Avenue
Newtown	Parkville
NSW 2042	Vic 3052

Details of upcoming conferences, study days and courses in Australia may be found in Christian magazines such as *On Being* or *Briefing*.

United Kingdom
Department of Extension Studies

St John's College
Chilwell Lane
Bramcote
Nottingham
NG9 3DS

Details of upcoming courses and conferences of relevance in the United Kingdom may be found in journals such as *Renewal* and *Alpha*.

Appendix: Apologetics and Theological Colleges

How do the approaches and ideas developed in this book relate to the world of theological training for ministry? I write as one who has worked in theological colleges for much of his ministry, so I can claim to know something of their strengths and weaknesses. It is my conviction that very radical changes need to take place in the patterns of training that we have come to take for granted.

First, it would be helpful if theological seminaries stopped playing at being universities. Their teaching often takes the same form as university teaching. It is often carried out by tutors with an academic bent of mind, who would prefer to be teaching in university contexts, had they been able to find jobs there. The academic year is patterned on the university year, with long vacations. And the practical experience to which students are exposed is pathetically small.

Moreover, the standpoint from which the academic teaching is done often shares in the secular presuppositions of the university, where the biblical material is often seen as a collection of merely fallible human documents, recording human convictions about God in different ages. That is emphatically not what the teaching of the Christian community is about. The result is that students often emerge with a serious schizoid tendency in their attitude to the Bible. They know in their hearts and from their devotional lives that it is in some sense the word of God. Yet they think that they know from their studies in the (generally sceptical) literature of the subject that it is full of errors. So what are they to teach their congregations?

There are other problems. There is little team-teaching in many colleges, and as a result students tend to be trained to keep doctrine, prayer, worship and so on in different mental compartments. They can emerge without any integrated overview of theology, just as they emerge with little or no experience of sharing it with others. Who would train engineers, teachers or doctors in such a manner? There is a great need for radical reform.

It would be very helpful if the training lasted for eleven months of the year. We have seen in a previous part of the chapter how well the New Churches make use of the time in training their upcoming leaders, and how much they can pack into a single year's preparation. Think how much we could do with two years! And think how it could relieve the funding problem, which is now threatening to bring the whole system to a grinding halt.

It would be advantageous if much of the training was on the job, rather than in the classroom, and if it took place under competent practitioners rather than under theoretical academics. Both have their place, and both are needed if we are to prepare people properly for the increasing challenge of ministry in a largely non-Christian society.

Furthermore, there needs to be a major concentration on apologetics and evangelism in the classroom. Tutors need to be recruited who are not only able to teach, but to take students out with them, and practise these two disciplines. I have made it a rule for my students at Regent College, Vancouver that nobody should graduate from the course without having been out with me in evangelising, and standing up to the objections of those who did not believe the Christian faith.

This immediately had three effects. It raised the profile

of the subject. It equipped people on the job. And it brought about a climate of intercessory prayer, an awareness of the spiritual battle, and carefully-honed preparation into the college, as people prepared to go out on mission. The sad thing is that few colleges today teach apologetics or evangelism, and even fewer have their instructors go out with their students into the chill winds of the agnostic world to learn by doing. When you do that, it transforms a college!

Finally, my longing would *not* be to see apologetics and evangelism tacked on as two further subjects at which long-suffering college staff are urged to have a go. Anyone engaged in theological education will know of the relentless pressure to add this and that subject to an already overcrowded curriculum. My goal would be to *see all subjects taught with evangelism and apologetics in mind.* In other words, how can what is taught be made relevant to those who are outside the faith? That is the question that tutors should ask themselves, in teaching their subjects.

The study of Augustine would be revolutionised if students appreciated that the barbarians are at our gates today, just as much as they were at the gates of Rome in the fifth century. His priorities for Christian ministry make sense today! The study of Gnosticism could spring to life if it were seen as a major precursor of the New Age. Arianism would mean a lot more if it were related to the tenets of the Jehovah's Witnesses. And a doctrine like justification by grace through faith could be enormously sharpened if it were contrasted with the legalism of so many contemporary cults – not to mention the assumptions of many church members! The Church has a right to expect this sort of training from its theological colleges – deeply grounded in God's revelation, yet carefully and imaginatively applied to the Church and the unbelieving world into which the students will go and minister.

Index